Roger Hollan

Captain Tom Hickman. *Photo courtesy of the Texas Ranger Hall of Fame and Museum, Waco, Texas.*

The
GENTLEMEN
in the
WHITE HATS

Dramatic Episodes in the
History of the Texas Rangers

by

C. L. DOUGLAS

STATE HOUSE PRESS
Austin, Texas
1992

Library of Congress Cataloging-in-Publication Data

Douglas, C.L. (Claude Leroy) , 1901-
The gentlemen in the white hats : dramatic episodes in the
history of the Texas Rangers / by C.L. Douglas.
p. cm.
Originally published: Dallas, Tex. : South-West Press, c1934.
Includes index.
ISBN 0-938349-81-3 (hardcover : acid-free paper)
ISBN 0-938349-82-1 (papercover : acid-free paper)
ISBN 0-938349-83-X (limited ed. : acid-free paper)
1. Texas Rangers—History. 2. Indians of North
America—Texas—Wars. 3. Comanche Indians—Wars.
4. Frontier and pioneer life—Texas. I. Title.

F391.D73 1992
976.4—dc20   92-6950

Printed in the United States of America

STATE HOUSE PRESS
P.O. Box 15247
Austin, Texas 78761

To

SEWARD R. SHELDON

CONTENTS

LIST OF ILLUSTRATIONS

FOREWORD

In 1934 when C.L. Douglas completed *The Gentlemen in the White Hats,* his highly readable chronicle of the Texas Rangers' deeds of valor, there were far fewer books available on the subject than there are today. A quarter-century had elapsed since the prominent author Albert Bigelow Paine had published his notable and enduring biography of the famed Ranger Captain Bill McDonald, and Dr. Walter P. Webb's classic treatise was still in process. At the time, much of what was commonly known about the Rangers had its sources in the writings of popular novelists like Zane Grey and Max Brand, and in a wide array of pulp Westerns. Douglas, by vocation a journalist, devoted years of research to these historic lawmen with their aura of courage and resolve.

For over a century the Ranger organization had possessed a difficult-to-define mystique not held by any other such force across the world. Although the era and the location of its beginnings no doubt contributed in large measure to its mystique, one can nevertheless concede with little difficulty that the Rangers really were "a different breed."

All of us admire courage and hardihood, and even toughness if properly directed. These attributes were, of necessity, much more pronounced in those early days on the frontier; in fact, it is nearly impossible for today's average urban dweller to imagine the personal toughness and resolution made necessary by the everyday demands of a frontier society. Too, the Civil War had returned to civilian life a multitude of men long hardened to

ix

months and years of struggle and deprivation.

As perceived by Douglas, during the eventful fifty years spanning the westward expansion of the Texas frontiers, there had existed another war—an unforgiving conflict that pitted the vengeful Comanche Indian against the relentless advance of the white frontiersman and his ways of life. For two centuries the Indians had resisted with considerable success the intermittent intrusions by the Spaniards out of Mexico, but against the U.S. frontiersman it was to be a different story. This new intruder had the Indians outnumbered and outgunned. In this drama the Texas Rangers were to play a prominent role.

Many of the legendary feats of the Texas Rangers in this drama were again brought to life by Douglas, such as the feats of Sul Ross, who began his career as a Ranger in 1858 when he was only nineteen. He and several other members of the local militia accompanied a troop of the U.S. Cavalry, under Major Earl Van Dorn, on a sortie along the upper Brazos River where they attacked a hornet's nest of Comanches led by the wily war chief Buffalo Hump. Sul's first battle came near to being his last as well—he suffered from the ill effects of a heavy rifle ball through his body for the rest of his life—but two years later, as a Ranger Captain, he led a similarly violent engagement against another Comanche village on the Pease River. In this noted battle, Ross and a Mexican escort killed the Indian leader Peta Nocona and then brought Nocona's wife, the long-lost captive white girl Cynthia Ann Parker, back to civilization.

Herein narrated are more than just tales of Ranger courage against the Indians. The tale of Captain Lee McNelly who, despite an early death at age thirty-three from tuberculosis, broke the power of General Juan Cortina, the "prince of the Mexican cattle thieves," is a stirring one. The exploits of Frank Hamer, called out of retirement to chase Bonnie and Clyde in a match of "old-time Ranger cunning against the shrewdness of the modern gangster," still captures the imagination.

Does the Texas Ranger mystique still persist? It does indeed. Almost every season witnesses the appearance of yet another worthwhile publication, among which *The Gentlemen in the White Hats* takes its rightful place. The splendid Texas Ranger Hall of Fame, completed at Waco in 1974, now offers in its library a broad and priceless treasury of published, documentary, and photographic research material on both the Ranger organization and on its remarkable cast of characters.

The mystique will continue, too, as long as there are Texas Rangers in the mold of Ranger Captain A.Y. Allee. On the occasion of his retirement, Allee was being interviewed by a newspaper reporter who ventured to question him, "Captain Allee, is it a fact that on one occasion you attempted to arrest George Parr, down in Duval County?" To which impertinence the gruff old Captain's immediate response was, "Mister, I never *attempted* to arrest any man in my life—I either arrested him or I didn't arrest him."

And that is the way it was.

ROGER N. CONGER
Waco Historian
Former President, Texas State Historical Association
November 1991

CHAPTER I

Introducing
"The Gentlemen in the White Hats"

THERE are those who say that it was started by the Spanish—by the first of the Mexican conquistadores who came up from across the Río Grande to carve out a new empire in the wild and far-flung Land of the Téjas.

And there are those who have a different story, those who base their claims on the shaky foundations of pure legend—leaving history a plastic plaything in the hands of those who spread its inky trails across the records—but no one knows with any degree of certainty just where was first conceived the idea behind the Texas Rangers, that force of hard-fighting, fast-riding men, whose keen eyes have watched the fringes of a state's frontier for more than a hundred years.

Somewhere, among the scrap-ends that history has shuffled into the discard, the exact date of original organization has been lost. But what, after all, are dates but scrawling numbers used by the scribbler to lend authentic sequence to his work? Action, not numbers, counts for most and, to use the words of a famous captain in the old Frontier Battalion—"we will not count numbers if we fight."

What of the Texas Rangers and the history of the organization? This much is known—Stephen F. Austin mentioned "rangers" in letters that he wrote in 1821, but only in that casual, commonplace manner that you

1

and I would use in referring to the constable walking his beat in the next block. That, and nothing more. And so whatever valiant deeds were accomplished by the first of all the Rangers must be left to the imagination. History, in her cold-blooded way, has passed them by.

But this much is a matter of record—in 1835, when Texas was in revolt against the power of the Dons, a general council of Americans was called together to discuss protectionary measures, and out of this conference came plans for organization of the Rangers.

There were to be three companies of twenty-five men each—one to range east of the Trinity River, one between the Trinity and the Brazos, and one between the Brazos and the Colorado.

The man who enlisted in this force had his work cut out for him from the very start, for the council that organized the three companies had designated a common foe, the Comanche Indian; and it also named an objective, the removal of the fierce war-like tribe from the boundaries of Texas.

Thus, in the true analysis of the thing, the Texas Ranger owed his job to the Centaurs of the Plains, so-called because, when they swooped down on the scattered settlements, they sat their mustangs with the grace and ease of mythology's foremost horseman.

And so, before going into the story of the Ranger himself, let us arrange the "props" and set the stage over which he was to walk for more than half a century to come; let us, too, go behind the curtain and observe the arrangements for the play.

Once upon a time . . . many, many moons ago . . .

gray smoke curled from thrice a thousand tipis; great herds of fat buffalo, thundering westward, raised dust clouds on the swelling plains; and the smile of the Great Spirit rested on the Land of the Téjas.

For this was a happy hunting ground, and the people of the Comanche were well content—content to follow the path of the sun, to trail in the wake of the herds, and with unslung bows ride down the bellowing cows and take their meat with the feathered shaft of an arrow.

It was a land of peace and plenty, a paradise of the prairies—as old Sleeping Wolf well knew as he sat in his lodge among the elders of the tribe. But Sleeping Wolf, poker-faced, flint-eyed, and with a single eagle feather in his hair, was thoughtful as he squatted cross-legged on the floor of his tipi. In his youth he had lifted Spanish scalps in Durango, and in his day he had barbed Apache breasts in the west, but he thought not of these things.

The old brave, on that day in 1795, mulled over ancient tales—tales that had come from his father and his father's father before him; traditionary history handed down by word of mouth from the time when the Comanche was a part of the Shoshoni of Wyoming; a tribal division beaten back into the mountains by the hostile Sioux and then driven steadily southward by the same pressure.

Through the years and through the generations the knowledge of that persecution still rankled—even here in Texas—though the Sioux were far away. But old Sleeping Wolf or Guikati, as he was more properly called, considered history in the light of present welfare. Perhaps, after all, the enforced move southward had been for the best. Unharassed by enemies, except for straggling bands of Apaches that dared invade the region from the west, this was a land of peace, plentiful in buffalo meat, and wide enough of range to give the Comanches their title as "wanderers of the plains."

This was their land, their own country—theirs to have and to hold—and with a zeal almost amounting to fanaticism they intended to hold it. True, there had been trouble from the south. The Spaniards, more than once, had crossed the Comanche frontier and had met resistance; and the warriors of the tribe had retaliated with such frequent raids across the Río Grande that they were as well known in the Bolson de Mapimo of Chihuahua and in Durango as they were on the plains of North Texas.

The Comanche had grown strong since the time of his exile from the hunting grounds of the North. How strong? Ask the Spaniards across the Río Grande—ask the few settlers who had dared show their white faces on the westward bank of the Mississippi!

Old Sleeping Wolf thought on these things as he sat on the floor of his tipi, and then he spoke:

"Old men," he said, his facial features as immobile as the expression on the face of a statue, "the Comanche has been on these plains for many moons. It has been our hunting ground and none has come to turn us from our lodges."

His black eyes took in the circle of Indians who

squatted about him, and as several strange faces came within the range of his vision, he continued:

"But a new people have come amongst us. They call themselves the Kiowa and they ask to share our hunting ground. They are strangers, and yet they are not strangers. They are our brothers, because, like our own people, they have been driven from the buffalo runs of the North by the Sioux." He hesitated, and then went on: "They would make their lodges among our lodges and hunt with us, and make war with us when war is to be made. Will the old men of the Comanche speak?"

A deep silence, broken only by children playing in the village street, blanketed the tipi—and then a lesser chieftain, who had been plucking at the tufts of a buffalo robe, began an oration. For an hour he spoke in the sing-song tongue of his tribe, holding forth upon the glories of the Comanche, their prowess on the hunting field and on the war path. And when he was done, still other Indians spoke.

For long and weary hours the council went on in the tipi of Sleeping Wolf, for lengthy talk is the way of the Indian, but when the last word was uttered, by sign and tongue, there came from the lodge the famed unwritten Kiowa-Comanche Confederacy of 1795, a verbal treaty that was to stand through a hundred years of white invasion—a pact that remains unbroken even to this day, though tribes are shattered and their remnants cast upon the mercy of those who killed their buffalo and drove them from their land.

It is a theory that may be error, but after a study of Kiowa and Comanche history as it relates to the early settlers of Texas, I have come away with the distinct feeling that the idea—or at least the nucleus of the idea —that gave birth to the organization known as the Texas Rangers really germinated that morning in 1795 in the lodge of Sleeping Wolf.

For out of that sinister and portentous confederacy came one of the finest divisions of light cavalry the world has ever known—a contingent that was to be a rankling barb in the side of civilization for many years to come. Half-naked, untrained, and armed only with the crudest weapons, but at the same time dashing, bloodthirsty and bold, these men fought for a cause—for possession of a domain they had come to consider as their own. And in this a true Comanche was as fanatically zealous as the Madhi of Allah, as cruel as a Barbary buccaneer, and as recklessly daring as Sir Launcelot du Lake. He rode like a Centaur, lanced like a knight, and twanged arrows with the accuracy of a rifleman.

And when the first white settlers began edging themselves over the corners of the Texas plains the Comanche struck . . . thus setting the stage and calling the cue for the appearance of the Texas Ranger.

The general council of Texas, when it met at San Felipe de Austin in 1835, knew the enormity and the seriousness of the task ahead; but knew, too, that the embryo colony had in its midst many men of pioneer stock capable of coping with the situation—hard, adventuresome men who counted danger not a fly; in fact, courted it, and liked it. So the muster list in the first Frontier Battalion was quickly filled—with men who could ride like Mexicans, trail like Indians, shoot like outlaws, and who—like the Comanches themselves—didn't favor the capture of prisoners. A hard lot, these seventy-five who set out in 1835 for the scouts on the Trinity, the Brazos and the Colorado to risk their scalps for a salary of $1.25 a day.

They were the first. Others, down through the center of a century, followed on their trails . . . guardians of law and order, makers of peace, but above all, Nemesis for the Kiowa and the Comanche.

They carried on their saddles a carbine or a musket, and on their belts a brace of heavy pistols, together with a long keen knife—tools with which to carve out the destiny of a new country. They were undrilled, and they were un-uniformed, except for high boots and the big white hat, which is to be found in the dress equipment of almost every Ranger.

They were individuals, and they fought that way—and they made a good job of it.

I shall not attempt to tell a full and detailed story of the Ranger service, for that is a task seemingly beyond the limitations of human possibilities—a work that would require the concentration of a Gibbon and the skill of a Plutarch—and so I shall be content to present this narrative from the background of certain personalities as they pertain to the epoch of Texas history in which they moved.

But this word of warning . . . It is not a pretty tale; not a romance for the faint-hearted and squeamish patron of a patent-leather civilization. It is rather, a tale of blood, and war, and death.

I give you—The Gentlemen in the White Hats!

CHAPTER II

Captain Coleman and the Earlies

CAPTAIN COLEMAN was a lusty lad, as handy with his fists as with a gun—and when he swung the scalping knife the hair peeled away in a single mat.

An accomplished man in more ways than one, this former Kentuckian who had fought in the siege of Béxar with a long squirrel gun, a Bowie knife and a powder horn. High-strung, brave, and with an excess of daring in his system, he loved a fight on any ground and with any weapon. Back in Kentucky, where he had cut his teeth on a musket barrel and used a shot pouch for a rattle, he had drilled his first hole in an Indian hide at an age when most modern boys are thinking of their first air rifle.

A rare-plucked man, the Captain—black-eyed, mustached, tall and silent—and so, when President David G. Burnet of the Republic of Texas sat himself down to consider the officer personnel of a Ranger force to move against the troublesome tribesmen in the north, he wasn't long in reaching a decision.

The hostile Comanche and the Kiowa, jealous of white invasion, were on the raid again, and what better man than R. M. Coleman of Bastrop to put the savage in his proper place?

Accordingly, in the year 1836 Mr. Coleman received from President Burnet the first captain's commission issued in "The Mounted Riflemen of the Ranging Serv-

8

ice," along with orders to raise twenty-five men and proceed to the Trinity and upper reaches of the Brazos to see what he could do about knocking down the redskins' ears.

Captain Coleman knew what he was about and, as he went about organization of his command, he laid down but one set of requirements—

"Each man," he specified, "must report with a serviceable horse, a good rifle and a brace of pistols."

That was all. He said nothing about courage, that virtue being more or less taken for granted in those days —and besides, a man's application for Ranger service was proof enough of courage. The muster rolls soon filled. Adventure-minded young men reported from San Antonio de Béxar, from San Felipe de Austin, from Bastrop, from all the country 'roundabout, and within a few weeks Captain Coleman and his hearties were off for the frontier to puncture hostiles. He had one definite mission.

"Let us," said President Burnet, "give the Comanches a scare that they will remember. Let us show them that the Texans mean business; that raids on the outlying settlements won't be countenanced."

And that is exactly what Captain Coleman did. His frontier expedition crossed the Trinity River, penetrated to the falls of the Brazos and then moved on to the Colorado, and though they evidently encountered no large war parties, they met with groups of stragglers all over the area. It was a touch-and-go, boots-and-saddles sort of campaign; a sudden encounter of the plains, a chase and a game of hide-and-seek across the hillocks,

and then a few spurtles of fire and a few wisps o' smoke
—and a clean-up party to take the trophies, the war
shields, the lances and other bits of accouterment with
which the Indian rode forth to battle: Wild, free days
with danger riding at the elbow and death hanging at the
stirrup straps!

And at length Captain Coleman came home from the
wars to make his reports, but just what words the
Captain used to describe the success of his campaign
nobody knows, the records of his engagements having
been among those destroyed when fire gutted the adjutant general's files in 1855. But one may well assume
that they were as brief in content as the taciturn spirit
of the Captain himself . . . but no man needed reports
who came home with a string of scalps tied to his
saddle skirts.

But what of the other companies—how had they been
amusing themselves while Captain Coleman and his
merry boys had been cutting such a wide swath through
the upper regions of the state? They had, indeed, been
pursuing about the same type of pleasures in other
localities. Captain G. B. Erath and Captain W. M. East-
land, operating in the vicinity of Cameron, had indulged
in several gay and sanguine parties with the wily redskin, but had come away with two casualties. But for
the two men killed they had, in a single battle, knocked
over fifteen Comanches to even up the score.

That same year, however, saw the end of Captain
Coleman's service with the Rangers, a heated quarrel
with General Sam Houston precipitating him back into
civilian life in 1837 . . . for then, as now, politics some-

times cropped up in the service. But the first of them all didn't have long to regret his enforced inaction. A few months later he died, but not as might be expected, with his boots on. While on a trip to Velasco, near the mouth of the Brazos, he was drowned while bathing in that stream.

He left behind him on a farm near Bastrop a wife, three sons and two daughters, and the tragic fate which befell them was, ironically enough, typical of a condition against which the Captain had been fighting so hard . . . an incident which put the Rangers on the trail again and, strange to relate, gave the Comanches a possible warrior of the Captain's own blood to make war against his successors in the years yet to come.

Mrs. Coleman and her six children—two girls, fifteen-year-old Albert, four-year-old Thomas, and two older boys, James and Roger—were engaged in cultivating the prairie on the outskirts of the little settlement that had sprung up about the present site of Bastrop, and since the Captain's death they had found the task somewhat difficult. On February 18, 1839, Mrs. Coleman, with the two girls and Albert and Thomas, were hoeing in a field two hundred yards from the cabin where they made their home. James and Roger were in a near-by belt of trees gathering wood. It was a warm and peaceful morning and the little group in the field talked and joked as they went about their work.

But suddenly there was a warning shout from Albert. He had seen something in the edge of the wood, the flash of a feathered head and the glint of a brown body, and Albert needed no second glance to tell him that the

Indians were on the raid. And they were. Yelling like wild men, they charged out across the field—a hundred Comanches, out for blood and determined to make a kill.

The race for the house began, and all would have gone well, perhaps, had it not been for Thomas. The chubby legs of the four-year-old couldn't keep stride with those of his elders and Thomas was far behind when Albert reached the cabin door and flung it open for his mother and sisters to enter. The girls got safely in but the mother, suddenly seeming to remember Thomas, stopped as though to return to him. Through her eyes there flashed but one brief scene—her baby struggling in the arms of a warrior—and it was the last thing that Mrs. Coleman ever saw. In the next second she fell through the open doorway . . . the barbed shaft of an arrow through her throat.

All through that long afternoon, while the two weeping girls tried in vain to remove the arrow from the body of their mother, young Albert, using one after another of the three muzzle-loading rifles in the cabin, fired slug after slug through the window at figures lurking in the clearing; and once in awhile, as he heard the tell-tale plunk of a lump of lead, he would smile grimly to himself as he swabbed the long barrels with a ramrod. A true son of his ranger father, this fifteen-year-old Albert. Some day he might have led a company of his own had things been different.

The afternoon wore on, and Albert wondered what had become of James and Roger. Had they been massacred in the wood, or had they broken through the hostiles to carry the alarm into the settlements? It was not until late evening that the answer came, but Albert never knew. For near sunset a slug from a rifle-armed warrior had torn away half of Albert's chest, and he lived only long enough to warn his sisters against answering any calls unless they were first certain that white men were outside the cabin.

James and Roger really had slithered through the line. The white men they brought back to the cabin found four dead warriors in the clearing, mute testimony that Albert had had his father's eye. The two girls were safe, but nothing ever was heard of the baby. What became of little Thomas? Who knows? Perhaps—like so many other children of the frontier—he became a Centaur of the Plains, to carry the gage of battle to Rangers who would follow on his father's trails, to ride side by side with the men who had put an arrow through his mother's throat.

The incident aroused the settlements. Within a few hours Captain Joseph Burleson had mustered fifty-two men and had set out for the north in pursuit of the marauding band, catching up to the fugitives early next day. There was a running, desultory fight and Joseph Burleson, bearing down on a brave in flight, was shot and killed only a few minutes before his brother Edward arrived with a reinforcing party of thirty-two men.

Through the day the ragged fighting line of mounted men moved across the prairies and the Texans took a heavy toll before night descended and aided the Indians in their escape. But that night of fighting did something to Edward Burleson. When he rode home next day he went with an indomitable hatred of the red man and everything he typified. Thence forward from that day it was an unfortunate "first American" who crossed the path of Eddie Burleson, as you will find in later chapters.

But before we meet this man again, down on the banks of the Nueces, other "captains courageous" must rove the plains.

For about the time that Burleson was riding home from the Bastrop country, Captain John H. Moore had dropped his calling card in a Comanche village on the San Saba. The Captain, on his pop call, had prepared for a short but lively visit, having with him fifty-five Rangers, forty-two Lipans and twelve Tonkawas, and a short and lively visit it was. The Comanches, so it happened, were just spoiling for a fight, especially when they observed that Captain Moore had buddied up with their hereditary enemies, the Tonkawas—and they let the Rangers have it, hammer and tongs.

It was a right nice fight while it lasted, a sniper's affair conducted from horseback, but Captain Moore made a serious mistake. He picketed too wide when he camped for the night and in the morning his men discovered that the crafty aborigine had stampeded their horses in the darkness.

Captain Moore, a Tennesseean who came to Texas in 1821 and fought like the valiant soldier he was through the Revolution, was left stranded. He almost wore off the soles of his boots on the march back to the settlements.

The Captain, however, had his revenge. It was a very different story when, the following year, he raised a company of ninety men, including twelve Lipans under

Chiefs Castro and Flacco, and went scouting along the upper Colorado, near the present city of that name. He used a pistol shot and a cavalry charge by way of calling card this time, rode into a surprised Comanche village and cut down almost every warrior on the local census list. And instead of walking home, he brought back this time several hundred captured mustangs.

Moore had the satisfaction of carrying with him to his deathbed (he died in Fayette County in 1880) the knowledge that he had played no small part in President Mirabeau Lamar's program to exclude the Indian from Texas. Lamar, in carrying out his policy, had more or less peacefully chased the Cherokees, Delawares and Shawnees out of East Texas—but Captain Moore, for his part in the scheme of things, had used a different method. Some of Lamar's exiles came back.

Those whom Mr. Moore attended to couldn't . . .

The scholarly Mirabeau Lamar, with a strain of Gallic poetry in his blood, meant well no doubt, but he did bite off something of a large-sized chunk . . . as subsequent events were to prove.

The Comanches and their allies, the Kiowa, were related to the tribes of the East in about the same ratio as the tiger and the lamb; and if the fist of Texas was to smash the Comanche face the Comanche first intended to leave his teeth marks on the knuckles. In the light of this sullen determination on the part of Sleeping Wolf's bold descendants, the chronology of the Texas Rangers would be incomplete without some reference to the great Comanche raid of 1840. Although the Rangers themselves played but a slight part in the

principal action of the affair, it furnished them one of
the best seasons for bushwhacking in the history of their
organization.

CHAPTER III

The Great Comanche Raid of 1840

THE council house at San Antonio de Béxar buzzed with excitement. The tribesmen of the Comanches were coming in to make a treaty, and the Texas horizon was flushed with a promise of peace.

It was a gesture of their own making and Mirabeau Lamar, president of the Texas Republic at that time, January of 1840, had agreed to a conference. The poet-president, one of the strongest advocates of complete expulsion of the Indian from Texas, probably had a great many other cards up his sleeve, but these he kept strictly unto himself; but by that same token the chiefs of the Centaurs had a few rabbits of their own to drag from the war bonnets.

Lamar already had succeeded in chasing the Cherokees and allied tribes from East Texas—a move upon which he seemed determined—and so it is not unreasonable to assume that Lamar intended to go ahead with his program. The Comanches were different from the peaceful East Texas tribes, but even if they were to be kicked over the borders by the toe of a Ranger's boot, there was other work to be done first. The Comanches, in their frequent moonlight raids on the settlements, had kidnaped many children from the Texans—young boys and girls, even babies, whom they had carried back to their villages to foster and train in the ways of an Indian's life.

The tribesmen seemed to have an absolute mania for that sort of thing and it is a proven fact—as later chapters will disclose—that not a few baby Texans grew up to swing a tomahawk and ride with the Centaurs against their own people. That was the prime reason behind Lamar's agreement for a conference—to get back, if he could, some of those captive children. This done, the Indians could look to their own scalplocks. But the chiefs were not all fools; they knew where they stood, and the advantage that they held, as they straggled into San Antonio de Béxar to meet the representatives of General Albert Sidney Johnston, the Texas secretary of war.

The parley was of short duration. The War Department merely made it plain that no attempt would be made to negotiate a treaty until the Comanches felt generous enough to bring in their young captives and surrender them to their people. The chiefs were cagey; they palavered and they argued, but finally they agreed to meet the demand and return within two weeks.

Mighty were the preparations that President Lamar and General Johnston made for the second parley, the general ordering Lieutenant Colonel W. S. Fisher of the First Texas Regiment to proceed to San Antonio and hold himself in readiness to take the Indians captive if they failed to bring the prisoners. The soldiers waited, but the tribesmen took their own sweet time about gathering at the council house; in fact, it was not until March 19 that two Comanche runners appeared on the outskirts of San Antonio de Béxar to report the advance of sixty-five Indians from the plains.

Led by the famous Muke-warrah, the chiefs came in,
followed by a motley assortment of lesser braves and
a number of squaws and children; a moiling, jabbering
throng that filled the council room to capacity. Colonel
Hugh McLeod and Colonel W. G. Cooke, sent by
President Lamar as commissioners to negotiate with the
tribe, were direct and to the point.

"Where," they asked, "are the captives?"

Whereupon the chiefs singled out a thirteen-year-old
girl from among the children and led her before the
commissioners. Tanned as she was by the sun and the
wind, the child had escaped notice by the whites during
the preliminary proceeding, but now, as she stood
before the colonels, they saw that she was white.

"Where are the others?" demanded Colonel Cooke.
"We have definite information that there are many other
captives in your camps."

The chiefs shrugged their shoulders. The white men
had been misinformed; they did not trust their red
brothers; they doubted the truth of the Comanche
word. And that was all, except a low muttering among
the tribesmen. The two colonels, realizing that nothing
was to be gained through questioning of the Indians,
then took the girl aside for a private conference.

She said that her name was Matilda Lockhart,
captured some months previously in a raid, and she
made it plain that the chiefs had lied. That was all
Colonel Cooke and Colonel McLeod wanted to know.
They returned to the council room, told the chiefs what
the girl had said, and added that she had revealed their
plans for holding other captive children for ransom.

The muttering among the warriors was renewed and, taking advantage of the Indians' preoccupation, the commissioners ordered Lieutenant Colonel Fisher to move two companies of his troops into the council room. Silently, the soldiers trouped in, one company by the front door and one by the rear entrance, and as they lined up along two walls of the room the Comanches watched with burning eyes. They sensed, but too late, that they had been led into a trap. Then they heard Colonel Cooke speak:

"You see the soldiers," he said, as calmly as he could. "They are here to take you prisoner. Until you turn over to us the white children you have in your possession you will remain here in San Antonio . . . as hostages. I have nothing more to say."

The atmosphere of the council room became tense. The chiefs and the bucks sat rigid in their places, the squaws looked on with wondering eyes—even the half-naked children seemed to sense that they were about to become part of a great drama.

A danger-fraught silence settled over the council room and then—one of the chiefs rose from his place. With the eyes of the entire assemblage upon him he ambled, slowly and deliberately, toward the front door. But a soldier, with his rifle at the porte, barred the way. The chief's eyes flashed. Who was this upstart, this private soldier, to stand in his way—he, a chief, of the Comanche? The Indian's right hand went to his girdle. There was a flash of cold steel . . . a cry of pain . . . the blade of a knife was in the soldier's side!

Simultaneously, white men and red arose to their feet

with a scraping of boots and a shuffle of chairs. Hands went to the pistol butts and from here and there over the room came the snick of a musket hammer.

"Catch him ... somebody!" shouted a white man near the back of the room—and Captain G. T. Howard did. He grasped the Comanche chieftain about his royal neck and clamped down on the windpipe. But, in the twinkling of an eye, the chief whirled like a dervish, broke free of the captain's powerful hands, swung his already bloody knife in a wide arc, and slashed into the officer's abdomen. The captain, however, kept his feet, and his wits.

"Shoot him!" he ordered the sentry, and staggered to the wall.

The wounded guard fired from the hip ... and in less time than it takes for the smoke to clear a rifle barrel, one chief of the Comanche was stalking fat buffalo in the happy hunting grounds.

And then hell on wheels rolled through the council house of San Antonio de Béxar. There was a general drawing of knives in the Indian section of the house and, as the blades slipped free of the sheaths, those Texans who had snicked back the hammers of their rifles let go a stream of fire into the close-ranked redskins. Then the fight started in dead earnest.

The surviving Indians rushed and the lanky, mustached Texans, ranged against the walls, had no time to load again. It became a dirty, messy, short-range affair ... a brawling, hacking, slashing, bloody bit of work. The Texans used their pistols and then they clubbed their muskets and waded in to give the day a proper finish.

Women cowered on the floor and children screamed . . .
the smoky room became a gory shambles. In that
slaughter house that day at San Antonio de Béxar even
the walls were spattered with blood, and lead, and brains.

And finally, when the last Comanche war-whoop was
heard above the mêlée, the Texans stopped to take stock
and do a little morbid arithmetic. On the floor and in
the courtyard outside lay the bodies of seven white men.
Eight others were dressing down their wounds.

So messy had been the fight that in the cleanup there
was some trouble, at times, in determining whether a
casualty was red or white under the crimson coating of
his skin, but when the Texans made their final count
they stacked the remains of thirty-five Indians in the
street outside, and of this number thirty were warriors,
three were squaws and two were children who had been
trampled and mauled in the slashing engagement. One
hostile, and only one, made an escape—a half-breed
Mexican, who was last sighted leaving the precincts of
San Antonio with the little bees of bullets buzzing about
his ears.

Thus ended the "peace conference" of 1840 . . . with
the Texans holding prisoner two old men, twenty-seven
women and children.

What next? The Texans considered . . . and then
they hit upon a plan. They singled out one of the
captured squaws, gave her a message, and instructed
her to return to the tribal tipis. Briefly, the contents
of the message was this—if the Comanche would come
to San Antonio at once, bringing with them all the
white captives in their possession, an exchange could be

arranged. They must come, the squaw was told, under a white flag, and they must be quick about it.

One week later the white flag waved from a hilltop outside the city. The Comanche traded a dozen white children for twenty-nine people from their own tents, but at that the affair wasn't over—not by any means. The chieftains of the tribe went back to their lodges to brood, and plan reprisals.

And then Death rode the wind across the west of Texas. Like an avenging flame, it started on the plateaus of the north, swept o'er rolling prairies, and stopped only when the Comanches dipped their red-tipped lances in the Gulf.

Without warning they swept from Antelope Hills and the Panhandle country—a brown tide of a thousand, howling, naked savages, who burned homes, slew settlers, destroyed herds and seized loose horses as they went; and with the help of overpowering numbers and the invaluable aid of Señor Don Valentin Conaliso, general commanding the military in the north of Mexico, they reached to Linnville on Matagorda Bay.

This town they sacked, but the inhabitants, warned of their coming, fled to the bay in boats and let the Indians have the place. And they practically moved Linnville, lock, stock and barrel—loading 3200 stolen horses with loot from the settlers' homes. One old chief, who rode a horse decked with ribbon, found somewhere in the ruins a high silk topper and a claw-hammer coat. Wearing the hat, he put the coat on back part before, threw his naked legs over the back of a mustang, raised

an umbrella over his head, and thus attired went forth
to hunt down straggling Texans.

He still was wearing this unique ensemble when, a
day later, his body was dumped into the bay . . . the
chief had found his Texans, all right.

The great Comanche raid continued, and it gave the
Texas Rangers steady work for months to come. It
caused, in fact, a call for new recruits, for the tribesmen
split up into small bands for quick and bloody thrusts
at outlying communities.

One such kill-and-carry raid was made on the farm
of Johnstone Gilliland, situated on the Don Carlos ranch
in Refugio County. The band, led by a renegade white
man, killed Gilliland and his wife and carried away two
small children, Rebecca and William.

The Texas Rangers took the trail. A company, headed
by Captain Price and Lieutenant A. B. Hannum, overtook the murderers and kidnapers before they put
twenty-five miles behind them, and the Indians, seeing
the Rangers closing in, arrayed themselves in battle
formation, spreading out in a ragged line to wait
the attack.

Price halted the men to look over the ground and, as
they discussed the plan of attack, the Rangers witnessed
a strange thing. The old chief of the band, more bold
than cautious, walked out in front of his men and began
prancing down the battle line. He held in his hands
something that he put to his lips, and then out over the
prairie came the sound of doleful, choppy music. The
chief had a flute . . . and he played it like a Scottish piper.

There was in the Rangers, however, one man who

didn't relish such showy displays, and this man, Mabry B. Gray, called Mustang Gray, mumbled beneath his breath and said he'd make the redskin play an entirely different sort of tune; and Mustang Gray was in the van when the Rangers charged the line that day . . . the piper never piped again.

Price and his men routed the tribesmen and recovered the captive boy and girl, but the boy was seriously wounded . . . lanced in the side by the renegade white during the getaway.

This was only a sample of the work the Rangers had cut out for them as a result of the Great Raid of 1840, and the events which followed brought into prominence one of the greatest of them all . . . Jack Hays.

CHAPTER IV

Jack Hays ... First-class Fighting Man

CAPTAIN JACK HAYS didn't give a damn—he was built that way.

He liked a fight or a frolic as well as any caballero who ever swung two pistols from his hips; and the man didn't live that Jack Hays was afraid to go up against in any sort of rough and tumble. All told, perhaps, Jack put more names on the Comanche casualty list than any other Texas Ranger of his time, but it may be that there was a good and valid reason for his endeavors along this line.

Because when Mr. Hays, a tall, angular Tennesseean, crossed the Texas line about 1839 fresh from the surveying camps of Mississippi, he was doomed to meet with a bitter disappointment. He had heard about the fun to be found in the new republic, and being one who not only took his fun where he found it but went out to hunt it, he left his place among the road builders and hied himself to the Lone Star country.

By the time of his arrival, however, the Texans already had mopped up the Mexican army and since that job, primarily, was what he wanted to help with, he was a disappointed man. Naturally enough, he had to find some outlet for his pent-up fighting fervor, and since the Comanches were throwing all sorts of festive blood-letting parties in the west, Jack Hays found little difficulty in getting work to his liking. Already he had mastered the fundamentals of the gun fighter's trade, having studied the art somewhat extensively in the effete East, but it was in Texas that he was to develop the real finesse that was to mark him among the superior riflemen and pistoleers of his day.

When Jack first began to attract attention the battle of Plum Creek had been fought and won. General Felix Huston, Colonel Edward Burleson and Captain Matthew Caldwell and their men, catching the Comanche raiders on the rebound as they came from the sack of Linnville, had shattered the Great Raid of 1840 and had broken concerted power of the tribesmen. But, with the scattered bands roving the country, there was still plenty to occupy the attention of young men like the young Tennesseean.

And so Jack, who had distinguished himself somewhat by bumping off Indians and Mexicans in the vicinity of San Antonio, found himself, in the Fall of 1840, with a freshly-penned captain's commission in the Texas Rangers. Twenty-two years old at the time, our hero was naturally ambitious and rarin' to go. Thus it was that when he received his commission he glanced at it with one eye, whilst looking about with the other for some redskins to mess up.

He got his first chance down in the south of the state. A party of Indians had slipped in, stolen a remuda of horses, and bound for the plains, had skittered off toward the Guadalupe River. Here was a business directly down Jack's alley, and with twenty men at his back he galloped in hot pursuit, coming up to the war party as they prepared to ford the river. But right here the young Ranger captain received the surprise of his life—he had run up behind the pony tails of an even two hundred Comanche bucks, instead of the relatively small party he had expected to find. But that didn't stop Mr. Hays—not at all.

"There they are, boys!" he shouted. "Let's go and get 'em!"

And away they went—like smoke wraiths in the wind —with a clippety-clop and a ki-yi-yi! The thundering thud of the horses' hoofs and the shouts from the throats of the Rangers probably did more than bullets and gunfire to start the rout which followed, for the first rush was decisive and victory was an easy thing.

Flushed with his first success, Captain Hays immediately started looking about for new worlds to conquer.

He found one of these at Enchanted Rock. Hays and his men put behind them a few other similar encounters —quite enough to spread the Captain's fame through the Indian lodges—but now there had come a lull in actual hostilities and the government was employing Jack's good offices to carry out a surveying project between Llano and Fredericksburg. Hays and his men had no sooner gone to work than a war party, out on the loose and hearing that the surveyors were in the vicinity, rode over to size up the lay of the land. They found Hays himself separated from his companions and deciding that this was an opportune time to gather in his scalp—which they had been coveting for some time—gave the Captain the rush.

Hays, seeing no chance of regaining the camp, intrenched on Enchanted Rock and prepared to do battle. The Indians tried to climb the rock and haul him down, but discovered right away that they had treed a wildcat . . . for most of the lads bold enough to grapple with the granite incline slipped back down again and lay very still at the foot of the cliff. The two pistols and long rifle of Jack Hays caused a long round of wailing in the Comanche tents as a result of that day's work; and when Jack's command arrived to join the mêlée they put in enough pop shots to bring the day's casualty tally to fifteen warriors.

When Hays went back to Austin to report his varied doings he ran into something new—the Colt five-shooter, a stock of which firearm had been purchased by the Texas government but never used. Jack rather liked the feel of the new weapon and he asked permission to give the things an actual test on the frontier. The secretary of war said that it was quite all right with him; if Hays wanted to risk his life with newfangled devices, that was his own business. That's what Jack thought, too, and he gathered up a sackful of the revolvers and issued two for every man in his company. The men laughed, tucked the five-shooters in their belts, and rode forth.

We next find Captain Hays and company down on the River Frio, fresh from a chase and Captain Jack himself riding on a mule, his own personal horse having gone lame; and Jack and his mule were having difficulty in keeping pace with the forty-two others in the company. With our hero thus ridiculously mounted it pleased Fate at this rare moment to set two hundred Comanches on the trail ahead, and when the Captain saw them he seemed to forget, for the moment, that he might be improperly mounted for one of his great fame. Anyhow Jack, sniffing the enemy, shouted his familiar "There they are; let's go!" and the company was off in hot pursuit.

Hays dug his spurs deep, but the mule had a speed limit; the animal simply couldn't keep abreast the company, and the Captain saw himself in the disgraceful situation of meeting the enemy only to bring up the rear of the charge. He solved this difficulty, however. Noticing that one of his Rangers was sawing in on the reins, reluctant to give his horse the head, Jack shouted:

"What's the trouble over there . . . why don't you let that horse have his head?"

"If I do," replied the Ranger, "he'll run away with me. This hoss is hard to hold."

"Then let me have him," proposed Hays, "and I'll show you how to handle him."

And then and there he made the swap—mule for charger. But Hays, mounted on the animal, wasn't long in learning that the previous rider wasn't so far in error after all. The horse was hard to hold—and Jack, almost before he knew it, was out in front. Chief Flacco of the Lipans, and a good friend of the Captain, was right behind him, but even the Chief had to dig deep with the heels to keep the pace. Maybe Hays thought his men were immediately behind him, maybe he knew the true status of affairs, but the fact remains that he and Flacco —two lone riders—charged into the thick of the two hundred waiting on the prairie; not only charged, but broke the line and drove clear through, each riding with the reins free on the pommel and a spitting five-shooter in each hand! Not only that, they turned and rode right back, but this time the Indians, dumbfounded at the white man's daring, opened a lane and let them through. Then the company charged and put the foe to flight.

The five-shooter had been tested on the frontier, and it had been found wanting. Fast enough, this new revolving gun, but its slug lacked the force and the range that characterized the popular single-shot "hoss-leg."

Captain Hays was willing to discard "the damn things" before he set out to seek new combat with the Comanche. He certainly didn't use them a short time later when, farther down the river, he posted his men around an Indian-infested thicket and went in alone to beat the "game" out of the bushes. And Jack, had he been keeping a record, could have marked up eleven tallies in the book that day.

The year 1842 found the Hays aggregation protecting the Corpus Christi, Nueces and Río Frio areas, and they must have presented a fearful picture to the gentle redskin, dressed as they were in bear, buffalo and deer skins, some of them naked from the waist up. It must have been a colorful show, when on one occasion the company took part in a riding contest in which their opponents were Mexican vaqueros and a few tamed Comanches; but even with this expert competition first honors were carried away by Ranger McMullen. Long Quiet, a Comanche, took the second prize, the vaqueros not being in form that day.

The Hays company really had little time for this sort of sport. There was too much to do on the frontier.

It seemed they couldn't even go to town without running into trouble. For instance—Hays and his fellows happened to be scouting the outskirts of San Antonio in the fall of 1842 when General Adrian Woll, the French hireling of Mexico, slipped across the border, invaded Texas, and marched on the Alamo city.

It wasn't in the proper sense of the word, an invasion, for although the decisive battle of San Jacinto already had been fought and won by the Texans, Mexico and the Lone Star Repubic still were at war.

Woll had twelve hundred Mexicans under his command, and on September 11 he moved in on San Antonio, captured the city without resistance and without bloodshed, and took captive the district judge, the grand jury and all lawyers attending a court session then being held.

Frantic calls went out for the state militia and a courier rode through to Gonzales ordering Captain Matthew Caldwell to advance with the eighty men under his command and see what he could do about teaching the Frenchman a lesson.

But Jack Hays, who didn't think much of foreigners who went about attending to the affairs of other countries, didn't wait for Caldwell's men to arrive. The Ranger captain first wrapped himself in a Mexican serape, put on a straw hat, and, thus disguised, moved about the streets of the city, sized up the strength of the invading army and mapped out a program of battle. Then he rode into the outlying districts, mustered a force of about two hundred men, placed them in a suitable ambush, selected a small party of picked men, and rode up to the edge of the city.

Hays knew the value of heckling and, as he galloped about in gunshot of the Mexican lines, he and some of his more strong-lunged companions shouted all sorts of uncomplimentary things at their enemies from the south. General Woll was left to understand that he was a coward; that he was afraid to come out and fight in the open; and the more the general heard the more his anger increased. Finally, he could restrain himself no longer; and he ordered out his entire army to run down this impudent Texan, catch him if possible, and string him to the most convenient limb.

That was just what Hays had hoped for, and the trap worked perfectly . . . for, just as he led Woll's little army into the ambush, Captain Caldwell arrived from Gonzales with his own command of militia and several companies picked up along the way. Within the hour the Texans had the Mexican army heading south toward the border, but at Salado Creek they caught the fleeing troopers and gave them one of the soundest thirty-minute lessons in military tactics ever taught in the south.

The rout would have been a complete success except that through some misunderstanding Captain Nicholas Dawson and fifty-three men found themselves suddenly surrounded by the retreating Mexicans. They tried to fight their way clear, and did—but they left thirty-two men dead on the field of battle.

The flight continued to the banks of the Río Grande,

and, as they went, Jack and his men, galloping along with the militia, emptied one Mexican saddle after another before the invaders crossed the line to seek safety in the town of Mier. But even on the border some of the Texans could not be stopped, Captain William S. Fisher and his command of one hundred and seventy-six men crossing the river to attack the village on Christmas night. It was an unfortunate adventure for, after a brief battle, Fisher and his men, far outnumbered at the outset, were defeated and captured. The Mexicans immediately started them on the march to Mexico City but at the Haciendo Salado, near Saltillo, the party escaped.

That, however, only made matters worse because, when they were recaptured in the mountains four days later, General Santa Anna sent orders that one Texan out of every ten should be shot. Consequently, on March 24, 1843, Fisher's men were assembled to watch a Mexican officer drop one hundred and fifty-nine white beans and seventeen black ones in a large pitcher; and when this was done the Texans were ordered to draw.

Many of the Americans who had reached into the pitcher and brought out white beans, offered to trade with those who drew the black, but found no takers.

The seventeen holders of the blacks laughed and joked as they sat down on a log to face the firing squad . . .

Jack Hays and his men already were back in San Antonio, preparing for new scouts into the Indian country. They hadn't followed across the border this time, but the day was near when they would, although they didn't know it yet.

To detail the entire course of Jack's colorful career

would require a volume in itself . . . but it was Hays
who set the style for many a Ranger fight of the future.
Down on the Nueces in '44, he it was who passed the
word, as the Indians charged, to delay the fire and
"powder burn 'em when they're close enough;" and
it was Jack, in Gillespie County that same year, who told
his boys to keep their fingers off the triggers until the
Comanches came within striking distance with the lance.

Quite a lad, this Tennesseean who, when he stopped
chasing Indians, really had just begun to fight. For when
General Zachary Taylor came south in '46 to fight the
war with Mexico, Hays was so well known to fame that
he was requested to raise a regiment of his own picking
and join in the festivities. One can well imagine the kind
of regiment mustered by this twenty-nine-year-old
colonel (for he was now more prominently known as
Colonel John C. Hays.)

The men of his command, when they set out with the
American army for the Río Grande, wore pretty much
anything they pleased in the way of uniform—but the
artistry of the commander made itself evident in the
ordnance each man carried on his person. Every rider
in this regiment of Texas Rangers was equipped, in addition to his favorite type of rifle, with two single-shot
pistols, two six-shooters and a Bowie knife—fifteen shots
and a slash per man when it came to a fight.

Is it any wonder that they played so large a part in
the siege and capture of Monterrey? Is it any wonder
that the natives took them for a new type of savage, and
fled from them in terror, when they marched with
Taylor into the Mexican capital?

The war with Mexico at an end, Colonel Hays shook the dust of Texas from his boots. There is a faint suspicion that he was without funds—that he practically hitch-hiked to California where, in due time, he blossomed out with a sheriff's star in San Francisco. But fate looks after its own. Mr. Hays dabbled a bit in real estate over on the Oakland side of the bay, and he was enormously wealthy when, in the early '80s, he died— in bed.

But even while Jack Hays was on his way westward other Rangers were carrying the gage of battle across the Texas plains—men like Lieutenant Edward Burleson, and Captain Sul Ross.

Captain Jack Hays. *Photo Courtesy of the Steve Hardin Collection.*

CHAPTER V

*The Rangers Meet the Comanches
Knife-to-Knife on the Nueces River*

THE road to Laredo was lonely in those days because
few people passed that way—but this January morning
in the year 1851 was an exception to the general rule.
It was today a happy highway, and on the grass beside
it the morning dew glistened in the rising sun like
crystal gems.

The men laughed and joked as they rode, talked over
the fun they had in San Antonio de Béxar and framed
tales to tell their companeros when they came again to
Los Ojuelas, a Ranger outpost on the lower Río Grande.

But Lieutenant Edward Burleson, who rode at the
head of the thirty Texas Rangers, kept a wary eye on
the country through which they were traveling. As they
jogged along his mind was on other things than the
ribald jokes and snatches of new song picked up in a San
Antonio barroom. For he was a man to attend to his
business, was Edward Burleson. He had been through the
mill and he knew what it was. It was this same Edward
Burleson who had seen an arrow through the throat of
Captain Coleman's wife; who had seen his own brother
slain by Comanches while seeking to avenge the Cole-
mans after the Bastrop County raid. It was this same
Burleson who had fought in the battle of Plum Creek,
the fight that broke Comanche power during the Great
Raid of 1840. He knew the reward of keen eyesight and

wary senses . . . and this morning he and his men were
fated to reap that reward, for whatever it was worth.

They were nearing the Nueces, and the sun was high
in the sky; God was in His heaven and all was right
with the world—or, at least it seemed that way. But
it wasn't.

Over across the prairies Lieutenant Burleson saw
something, a few tiny specks on the horizon. He reined
in, lifted his right hand to indicate a silent halt, and
waited. The specks drifted nearer.

"Indians!" said Lieutenant Burleson to the man who
rode at his side. "Three of them."

Ranger Baker Barton turned in his saddle and, half
standing in his stirrups, passed the word back along
the line.

"Indians," he said, and that was all. The lieutenant
still was gazing at the horizon.

"Lyons," called Burleson, "what do you say . . . can
you make them out from this distance?"

Ranger Warren Lyons strained his eyes in the
direction of the three horsemen.

"Sure," he said, after a brief optical investigation. "If
they ain't Comanches you can write me down for a
Kioway."

If anybody knew, Warren Lyons did . . . for, captured
as a boy, he had spent ten years in the Comanche camps
and he knew a thing or two about the breed.

The lieutenant hitched up his belt, gave his maple
rifle stock an affectionate pat, and smiled to himself.

"That being the case," he said, "I guess we might as
well go after them. But we don't need thirty men to

catch three pesky Indians. I'll pick eight to go with me
. . . while the rest of you saunter on down the road and
rest your horses."

He tolled off his eight, including the aforementioned
Warren Lyons, and with a promise that he'd rejoin the
command within an hour or so, galloped away after the
three riders. The party, scouting through ravines, were
within five hundred yards of the trio before they were
sighted, but the Indians were well mounted and off like
the flash of a shot. It was an exhilarating chase through
the bright, crisp morning, the mustangs of the three
Comanches turning the earth under them like seasoned
racers, the hard-muscled legs of the pursuing horses
beating a rhythmic hoof tattoo on the rolling tundra.

Up hill, down valley . . . the Rangers leaning forward
in their saddles . . . the quarry riding free and easy like
the Centaurs for which they were named, swaying,
turning, flicking the single buckskin strand that looped
the mustang's foam-flecked nose. A mile . . . two miles
they ran, and the white men seemed to gain, enough
that Lieutenant Burleson pulled a pistol free of its holster
and held it muzzle up, ready to use as he came in range.

Three miles they ran, and then the Indians, suddenly
seeming to tire of the dangerous business, ran their
mustangs into a clump of woods and faced about with
a concerted war-whoop that could be heard even above
the thunder of the pursuing hoof beats. Burleson dug in
his spurs, waved his pistol above his head, and charged,
his eight Rangers behind him . . . but too late he saw the
trap he had entered.

The three Indians had dismounted and, joined by

eleven others who had been waiting in ambush, started twanging arrows into the onrushing Texans. William Lackey, who rode at the Lieutenant's left, saw a black spot which might have been a fast-flying bee—coming toward him. But it wasn't a bee. Ranger Lackey knew that; for he had seen the spot before. He tried to side-slip in the saddle, but too late . . . the arrowhead took him in the chest, pierced through his heart and came out below the shoulder blade. William Lackey toppled from his horse . . . one Ranger who would ride no more against the Centaurs.

Now, William Lackey was something of a favorite among the members of the company, and when Burleson saw what had occurred he reined in to a sliding stop, swung himself out of the saddle and ran to his fallen comrade's side. The other seven of the detachment also reined in, and with an utter disregard for their own hides, though the Indians were not more than twenty-five yards away, piled off to back the Lieutenant and throw a bodyguard around Lackey. And when it was discovered that Lackey was beyond all hope of human aid, it was too late to mount again. The fourteen Comanches had rushed.

In the first drive an arrowhead gritted into the ribs of Ranger James A. Carr, but as Carr felt the shaft penetrate his side he whirled and with one shot from his pistol dispatched a lancer who was bearing down on John Leach. Then the main action started—one of the bloodiest and hardest-fought, hand-to-hand combats in the history of the frontier, eight Rangers against thirteen braves. A horse screamed and fell, bleeding at the nostrils, to die in a pool of blood; and Ranger John Spencer, who in the first rush had received a lance point in the abdomen, dived in behind the dead animal, and with a Bowie knife in one hand and a pistol butt in the other, prepared to meet all comers.

Carr, with the arrow shaft still sticking in his side, had received another in the shoulder, but he kept his feet, firing and slashing as the enemy rushed.

Burleson, meantime, was having difficulties of his own. He had grappled with a husky warrior, and they had gone down together—rolling, clawing, scratching, each trying to get in a blow with the knife. And, at last Burleson won. Blood-soaked, he regained his feet and turned his attention to other quarters. Albert Tom was backed against a tree encircled by a howling group of savages. One rushed in with a lance, but Tom turned the weapon aside with his left arm and slashed in at the Indian's chest with the knife in his right hand.

Burleson knocked down one and Tom another, and then they went to the aid of Spencer who, though seriously wounded, had not moved an inch from behind his dead horse. It was at this point that Ranger Lyons, who had been mixing it freely in the vortex of the fight, heard good news.

The former captive understood the Comanche tongue and he had caught certain words above the shouts of battle.

"They are telling each other that they are whipped," he yelled to Burleson, "but they don't know how to escape."

That was it—the Indians had been caught in a trap

of their own making and didn't know how to get out of it.

They fought, in that clump of trees on the Nueces, until no Indian had strength enough to wield his lance, until the white men's arms were stiff from the swinging of the knife . . . and finally nine Indians, leaving five dead on the ground behind them, limped away to lick their wounds. It was then that the Rangers took stock of the day's work.

Besides Ranger Lackey, slain in the first rush, Baker Barton lay dead, an arrow shaft through his stomach. The seven survivors all were wounded, Carr more seriously than his companions. Had it not been for the tragedy of the affair, his plight would have been ludicrous . . . for Ranger Carr actually had four arrowheads implanted in his thick hide and he still was on his feet, shouting and cursing at the departing enemy.

The rest of the company had heard the firing and had come to investigate, but arrived too late for action. They buried Lackey and Barton among the trees, set a crude marker above the mounds, and then took the lonely road to Los Ojuelas.

—But they did not sing.

CHAPTER VI

Iron Shirt . . . a Knight in Armor

OLD Iron Shirt was a "big shot" on the plains.

He could spit into the wind and turn a bullet from its course; he could mouth a line of magic words and stop an arrow in its flight—at least he told his folk he could and they, of course, were ready to believe him.

Big medicine, this old Comanche chief—who wore about his immortal torso a cuirass of Spanish steel that some of his body-robbing ancestors must have stripped from the remains of one of Coronado's men. That's how he got his name—Iron Shirt.

Up in the Antelope Hills of the Texas Panhandle, where he lived among his people, Chief Iron Shirt—or Po-hebeto Quasho, as he was more locally known—had the citizens fooled. He possessed, he told his braves, a strange and subtle power. He was immortal; exempt from harm; no danger, great or small, could touch him. And Death . . . pouff! That he counted not a coyote's bark! Thus he, "Whattaman" Iron Shirt, ruled the roost —until the Texas Rangers and a handful of Tonkawas proved before the tribe that man's mortality is a very real and feeble thing.

But before delving deeply into Po-hebeto Quasho's checkered career—which turned out to be one of the most romantic in all the annals of the frontier—let us glance first at a page or two of contemporary Texas history.

After the Great Raid of 1840, with the subsequent break-up of Comanche power at the Battle of Plum Creek, the savage line had been pushed steadily in the direction of the Northwest; and Central Texas, thanks to such buckaroos as Jack Hays and his ilk, had been made a comparatively safe place in which to live.

The powder-burned Indian, chased from his southern hunting ground by the two-gunned Rangers, had retreated to the plains of the Panhandle to make a last stand against the ever-creeping tide of white invasion . . . and they made the Antelope Hills their greatest stronghold. But the Red Man hadn't forgotten. His expulsion from what he considered his birthright still rankled, and so in the light of every moon they swept down in small, bloodthirsty bands to pillage and to plunder, to kill and maim, and even if they could the score they held against the whites.

For this bushwhacking mode of warfare Antelope Hills was the Indian base. It had always been—even during the terrible May of 1836 when a war party had swooped down into Limestone County to raid the home of Silas M. Parker and carry away his nine-year-old daughter, Cynthia Ann, who still lived among the Comanches as the wife of Peta Nocona, the second chieftain of the tribe.

But through the years the raids had gone on. The northwest frontier of Texas now was getting a bitter dose of the same kind that the settlers to the south had known so well—and so the state took a hand in affairs.

Early in the year 1858 a bill was put through the Legislature at Austin which provided for the muster of a special frontier force of Rangers to operate against the high Comanche, with particular stress laid on Mr. Iron Shirt's warlike covey in the Antelope Hills. Two veterans of the Indian fighting service were chosen to lead the ambitious expedition—Colonel John S. Ford and our old friend of the Nueces free-for-all, Edward Burleson, now captain, if you please.

And so in the month of July a party of one hundred men—that number being considered sufficient to cope with the situation—set off for the hills, accompanied by one hundred friendly Tonkawas and Anadarkos under the leadership of Chief Placido and old Jim Pock-Mark. These "friendlies" were, in fact, picked up along the way—at the reservation agented by Captain Shapley P. Ross, father of Sul, near the head of the Brazos.

The legion of doom marched north—

As the sun sloped into the west in the late afternoon of July 11, painting the sky in vivid red and gold, Colonel Ford, riding with a pair of Indian scouts well in advance of the main party, topped a little knoll on the prairie. He reined in and shaded his eyes with his right hand. Off to the west, like a black blot on the face of the sun-seared prairie, a buffalo herd was on the move. The Colonel called an Indian to his side and asked him to confirm the thing he thought he saw, and the Indian agreed that the white man's sight was good.

The Colonel smiled to himself . . . there, beyond him on the plain, the Comanches were chasing buffalo. Safe for so many moons in their northern stronghold, where no white man had dared to show his face, they hunted unmolested. So secure had they been in their supposition that the white man would not venture northward, they had not even troubled to post a sentry on the prairies to the south.

Colonel Ford sent an Indian back to halt the main party and then, with his heart beating a little faster, he watched the Comanches on the hunt . . . riding devils who swooped down like a hawk into the crush of the herd to twang an arrow into the forequarters of a cow and then pull free again to dodge the riotous jam. Centaurs of the plains, indeed!

Children—these people—he told himself with a twinge of regret as he watched the scene before his eyes. And then he remembered the silent, bloody raids along the lower stretches of the Brazos. He rode back to his command. At sunrise he would attack.

That night there was silence in the camp of the Rangers and the Tonkawas. Not even a fire was lighted for fear of putting the quarry on the jump. Ford and Burleson sent out scouts and they returned to report a small Comanche village a mile over the knolls. The main camp, they agreed, must be farther to the north. The colonel and the captain conferred. They would rush the village in the morning, strike one swift blow, and then push on for bigger game.

To them that night came Placido, the Tonkawa chief.

"These people," said he, "are my enemies, and the enemies of my father. They have stolen our ponies, burned our lodges, killed our women. The Tonkawas ask but one thing of the white man . . . that they be allowed to lead the attack against the Comanches. The first stab belongs to us, and we claim it."

And in the morning, as the sun peeped over the Antelope Hills, it was the Tonkawas who led the van. They did their work so well that only squaws were left alive in the village through which they passed. The Rangers rested on their arms, but only for the moment. For when Placido and his braves had done with their Comanche sticking, away they went . . . buckety, buckety, the main village for their goal. But Antelope Hills received warning of the force moving against it, the Rangers having flushed one lone warrior several miles to the south of the village.

This brave, by dint of remarkable riding, outdistanced his Tonkawa pursuers, reached the village on a well-spent pony and spread the alarm. The Comanches were waiting when John Ford's Rangers and their allies rode up within sighting distance of the tipis. They had spread out in open formation battle line across the entire south border of the village and their attitude, as revealed to Colonel Ford through his field glasses, seemed to dare the enemy to come in where glory waits. Colonel Ford considered the lay of the land.

His Tonkawas were on the right. If he put them forward, let them advance before the Texas men, the Comanches might be tricked into believing this a racial business and then get a sudden, swift surprise as the Rangers tailed in behind the friendlies to clean up the left-overs of the initial rush.

But the Comanches were not to be so easily fooled; they had their eyes about them, and before he had advanced half a mile Colonel Ford realized that the villagers knew the nature of the force coming against

them. Two hundred yards from the Comanche line
Colonel Ford pulled up his men and there both forces
stood, each taking the measure of the other. There they
stood, undecisively, wonderingly, like two groups of
strange people gazing at one another for the first time.
A few wild yells went up from the Comanche line, and
the Tonkawas stirred restlessly in their place on the
right flank of the Rangers. They fidgeted, anxious to
wade in and have done with the bloody work ahead, but
Placido and old Jim Pock-Mark held them back.

And then the watching Rangers witnessed a strange
and wonderful thing.

Out from the Comanche ranks rode a lone warrior,
a long red ribbon streaming from his mustang's tail. He
sat bareback on his mount, his brown legs bare from the
hips to the moccasined feet. He wore in his hair the
single eagle feather, and on his face the red war paint
of his people. Strapped to the left arm was a shield of
tight-drawn skin; and in his right hand he clutched
a long white lance, barbed at the tip and streamered with
a red ribbon that matched in color the band that floated
from his horse's tail. And as he shook his shield and
waved his lance in defiance of the Tonkawas, his hereditary enemies, the morning sun glinted on the bright
steel of a Spanish cuirass that covered his breast.

Old Iron Shirt had ridden out to steal the show!

Slowly he rode back and forth between the two lines,
hurling verbal taunts at the hated Tonkawas. Sometimes
he stopped, glared at the Rangers, brandished his shield
and dared the pick of Texas to come and take his scalp
in personal combat with the lance. There were a few

hardy souls who wanted to go, but Colonel Ford, knowing the way of an Indian with a lance, held these in
check; but he did, at last, nod an affirmative to several
anxious-eyed frontiersmen who, impatiently, had been
fumbling with their trigger guards as they sat and
watched the show. Three rifles cracked . . . and Iron
Shirt laughed.

He merely spat into the wind, and uttered new pro-
nouncements on the ancestry of the braves among the
Tonkawa, including for good measure a word or two
for Anadarko ears.

The Texans felt ridiculous. Could it be that they had
missed . . . with buffalo guns at the close range of a
hundred yards! Impossible! But still Iron Shirt rode
the lines!

This time six rifles cracked, and six of the best marks-
men of Texas looked out over their rifle muzzles to
survey the damage they had done . . . and Iron Shirt
laughed again, seconded by an answering chorus from all
his tribe. Po-hebeto Quasho had not lied. His charm
held good, even against the white man's guns. He had
spit into the wind and the bullets had turned aside.
Big medicine!

It was the psychological moment and Iron Shirt was
strategist enough to know it. Raising high his lance, and
half turning on his mustang to rally his encouraged
warriors, he charged—straight at the Tonkawa line!

But old Jim Pock-Mark was waiting. He had heard
those words about the Anadarko. He leveled his rifle,
sighted down the long barrel, and, as the first Co-

manche arrows began to rain down on the Tonkawa ranks, pressed the trigger.

Iron Shirt swayed in his middle, straightened, and then plunged head downward to the prairie. The steel cuirass of the conquistador clanked as its wearer hit the ground. Po-hebeto Quasho lay very still, a gaping, ugly hole above one eye. His mighty medicine had failed!

One bullet had stopped a vicious charge; had turned the tide of battle before it really started. The Comanches took one look at their fallen idol, and then they turned and fled.

Then John Ford's Rangers charged, their buffalo guns taking heavy toll this time as the warriors fled across the rolling plain. It was a sniping retreat, a "fall-back and then strike again" sort of engagement, the Comanches adopting this ruse to give their women an opportunity to escape. But something occurred on this Panhandle retreat "from Mons" that the Rangers had not bargained for.

Peta Nocona, second in command of the Comanches —now first, but he didn't know it—had heard the firing and was galloping to the rescue; and just as the Rangers were congratulating themselves on a victory neatly won, Nocona arrived with five hundred howling men. He had come on the run for ten miles across the prairie and he burned with desire to avenge his shattered tribe.

Ford rallied his two hundred into a solid front and lined up again in battle array, this time outnumbered more than two to one, and with the Texans and their allies wearied by the fight. And again the two opposing forces lined up on the plain and waited for the other to take the reins of battle in his teeth.

And again the Comanches started it—with one of their boldest braves riding out with a lance to challenge the best man among the Tonkawas. This time old Placido, with the heat of battle still upon him, was not so reluctant as before. He selected a man, one of the boldest of his lot, and sent him out; and there, on the plains of the Panhandle, occurred something that would have brought a thrill to the blood of Sir Thomas Mallory himself. For knighthood that day was in its flower; it bloomed in that brief hour for the last time, perhaps, on the North American continent.

The Tonkawa brave rode out to where the Comanche waited on his pawing horse. And then they met—like a Sir Bors running a passage of arms with Galahad, riding heads down, with shields before them, and with lances at the couch. The Tonkawa kicked drumming heels into his pony's flanks, bore down. The Comanche swerved and took the lance point on his bull-hide shield; jabbed once himself but missed, and then swept by, to turn his pony's head and charge again.

The Rangers looked on fascinated . . . for it was, as Colonel Ford himself later described it, a tourney unequalled since the days of Arthur's court. They met again, shoulder to shoulder, with a terrific impact. Lance clashed on lance; the Comanche swayed and then rode on, a broken spear held in his hand . . . but the Tonkawa pony had no rider. He lay where he had fallen.

And then, with the shouts of his compatriots in his ears, another Comanche warrior rode out to defy the

enemy and call for single combat; and another Tonkawa
came out to meet him. Three times this thing occurred,
and three times no Tonkawa returned to join his brethren
in the line.

It was then that Colonel Ford ended the business by
issuing orders for the charge that swept the Rangers
and their allies down upon Nocona's men. Placido struck
from the right, Colonel Ford from the center, while
Lieutenant Allison Nelson, hitting like a sledge, drove
in from the left flank. Together, they literally ran over
Peta Nocona's howling warriors.

And when the charge was over the Antelope Hills
were dotted here and there with lifeless men. Ford
counted but a few losses of his own . . . but seventy-five
of the enemy "bit the dust" that day.

Po-hebeto Quasho was found where he had fallen, a
broken idol on the plains. The Rangers stripped off his
iron shirt and took it with them back to Austin. But
they did it reverently . . . for he was a brave man, a
gallant warrior who, had he been on the other side of
the fence, might have worn the ribbons of a hero.

Lawrence Sullivan Ross.

CHAPTER VII

Arrows in the Dust

PEASE RIVER was the devil's playground in the 'Fifties; one corner of a detached hell that stretched from the Wichita Mountains into a sea of grass and rolling plains to the southward. But God in His wisdom had splashed it with His brush when he had painted in the corners of His world—and the earth on the banks of the South Canadian had been splotched a dusky red, like sand washed with a fast, unfading dye; like dust sifted with an element not its own. Even the sun, sloping down to where the prairie met the sky, was like a blazing ball of fire. A land of bright dawns and crimson sunsets, this country on the Pease. Was this an omen? Well, perhaps . . . for blood is also red.

But Lawrence Sullivan Ross did not think of these things as he rode into the north; for this was his vacation —just the thing for a twenty-year-old young man tired of the routine in Alabama's Wesleyan University, and as he rode along that September day in 1858 he remarked to Major Earl Van Dorn that he was having the time of his life and that he would have something to tell the boys when he got back to school. And the major had replied that Sul was indeed a lucky boy; that not many lads of his age would be instrusted with command of one hundred thirty-five friendly Indians on an expedition into hostile country.

"I only hope we find a fight," said young Sul Ross.

"I think we will, all right," the officer assured him.
"That is, if we hurry."

They jogged along—one a major of United States
cavalry; the other a stripling receiving his primary
lessons in a school from which he was to graduate one of
the most famous of all the Texas Rangers, and with a
reputation that would make him governor of the state.

Behind them on this morning rode three companies
of cavalrymen, Major Van Dorn's own men, together
with a varied assortment of Caddoes and Delawares
loaned temporarily to Uncle Sam and the state by Sul's
father, Captain Shapley Ross, agent for the reservation
near the headwaters of the Brazos. Command of this
latter group was an opportunity for the vacationing
college student, and his father had been glad to see
him take it.

But why was this force on the move? The reason was
simply this . . . on the dawn of the day before two
Indian scouts had come to Camp Cooper, near Fort
Griffin, with the news of a thickly populated Comanche
village in the hills of the Wichita about ninety miles
from the post . . . a group of survivors, no doubt, of the
Iron Shirt aggregation which Colonel John Ford had
decimated a few months before at Antelope Hills. Major
Van Dorn had lost no time; he had sounded "boots and
saddles" and, with the scent of the game still fresh, the
hunters had taken the trail. One swift, decisive blow was
all they wanted and the Comanche would be eliminated
from the plains forever . . . but that had been the
ambition of every military leader in the Texas depart-

ment before, and after, Major Van Dorn. The Comanche came of a wily breed.

As they rode along the officer appraised the boy beside him. Tall, slender, and eager-eyed, Sul Ross appeared to have the kind of stuff that frontier men are made of. Perhaps, after he had graduated next year from Wesleyan University, he would return and make his mark in this wild land as his father had done before him. A chip off the old block, thought the major, thinking of the captain down on the reservation.

"I suppose that when you finish school you'd like to follow along after your father," ventured Van Dorn, eyeing his companion askance. "A great fighter, your father . . . everybody on the frontier has heard about that scrap in Bell County."

Yes, young Sul knew all about that . . . how his father and three others had flushed an equal number of Indians and how both sides, finding their powder wet after a morning ride in the rain, had dismounted to fight it out with clubbed rifles and Bowies. He knew how the captain and Big Foot had come together, and how his father had grasped the chieftain's braids, killed him with a knife, and then had lifted off the scalp. An old story, but Sul wanted glories of his own. He said so . . . and the fairy of fighting men must have been listening.

Young Sul wasn't long in getting what he sought . . . just twelve hours, to be exact. For on the morning of the third day out from Camp Cooper, Ross and his Indians, who had been sent forward on an advance scout, rode squarely into the camp of old Buffalo Hump, whose bloody deeds along the border had made him one of the most hunted personages on Uncle Sam's long list of wanted raiders.

But Sul seemed to know exactly what to do. He had caught the enemy afoot and so, while his Caddoes and Delawares opened a sniping engagement, he took a small party and proceeded to rout the Comanche ponies. But the Comanches themselves hadn't run. Ever resentful of the interference of reservation Indians in their affairs, they dug in immediately and began dishing out some bitter medicine to the Delawares and Caddoes, the hostile riflemen zipping one volley after another down the shrub-covered ravines, then reloading while their less fortunately armed brothers held off attack with a rain of well-directed arrows.

Thus, when Major Van Dorn's "long knives" reached the scene of action the first desultory skirmish had developed into something entirely different. It would have been a foolish man who kept his horse in that mêlée, and so Sul's Indians as well as the Major's men tumbled off and began a creeping advance up the draws, pressing the enemy so closely that hand-to-hand and knife-to-knife encounters became the fighting mode of the moment. And in one of these Sul himself figured prominently.

With a Caddo at his side and a rifle in his hand, he had thrown himself into the thick of the fight—in a foggy, smoke-filled ravine where his men were advancing from bush to bush and taking, as they went, pop shots at Comanche heads as they appeared over near-by knolls. Unmindful of the bullets that whistled about his head, Ross rushed to the head of his column, squatted behind a rock, cocked back the hammer of his buffalo gun, and peered into the smoke-laden atmosphere. If only he could spot old Buffalo Hump himself and put a slug into his hide—then he would have something to tell the boys about. A figure moved in the bushes off at the right. Sul knelt, threw his rifle to his shoulder and looked down the sights, his finger already on the trigger. And then he hesitated, amazed by what he saw.

Just emerging from the trees, like one dazed and uncertain which way to turn, came a child—a white girl, about eight years old, and with a mass of blond hair tumbling about her shoulders; She was half naked and she looked, Sul thought, like a frightened deer. What was she doing here in the Wichitas; in the midst of a fight with the hostiles? A captive, perhaps . . . but Ross had no time to ponder over the question. A slug, swishing pased his head, reminded him of that. He turned to the Caddo beside him.

"Catch the white girl," he ordered. "Take her to the rear and hold her for me."

Not until he saw the Indian gather the child in his arms did he again turn his attention to the battle that roared about him, and when he did he became suddenly aware that another figure had taken up position on his left. There, not ten yards away, stood Mohee, tallest and bravest of Comanche braves—and Mohee was raising his rifle to the shoulder! Young Ross whirled, fired from the hip . . . and missed. Mohee, a dark smile on his face, did not hesitate. He pulled the trigger.

The world seemed to topple down on Sul Ross. He felt a sharp, agonizing pain under the ribs, and in the next second he fell, a gaping wound in the side. He lay still for a moment . . . tried to rise . . . but couldn't. And then he realized the reason why—his entire left side was paralyzed. With his good right hand he attempted to reach his pistol, but it was under him.

And then, like a trapped animal, he watched the Indian. Mohee had drawn a butcher knife from his girdle.

Slowly the Comanche advanced . . . a yard, two yards, three yards, and then . . . an ear-splitting explosion that seemed to rock the ravine from side to side. Mohee appeared to collapse at the waist. The butcher knife slipped from his clutching fingers. He fell on his face, his stomach riddled with buckshot.

"Got him . . . with both barrels!" said Lieutenant James P. Majors of the Cavalry. This much Sul heard, and no more. The roar of battle faded in his ears; the world went black before his eyes.

When Ross regained consciousness a medical officer was working over him. The fight was over, Major Van Dorn's men having routed the savages and driven them back into the hills. Several cavalrymen had been killed and wounded, and a few of the friendlies . . . Lieutenant Cornelius Van Camp was dead, an arrow through his heart, and the Major himself had been wounded . . . but they had left fifty-six Comanches on the field, and had burned a hundred lodges.

Ross asked the surgeon about the little girl. Yes, she was safe, but she didn't know her name; she didn't even remember when she had been captured.

"Then we'll call her Lizzie," said Sul, thinking of the girl he was to marry. And Lizzie Ross she became.

When the troopers carried him back to his father's reservation to recover from his wound the little girl went with him, and when Sul was up and about again he put Lizzie in school and returned himself to Alabama to complete his studies at Wesleyan. His vacation was over—and he had plenty "to tell the boys."

Sul Ross didn't forget the wound he had received in the Wichita campaign and so, after he had graduated from Wesleyan and had returned to Texas in 1860 . . . a battered veteran at twenty-two . . . he was more than glad to accept from General Sam Houston, governor at the time, a proffered commission as captain in the Texas Rangers. The Comanches were giving trouble in the north again and Governor Houston thought young Sul just the man to raise a company of sixty men to take the field against Peta Nocona, who at the moment was making life miserable for settlers along the River Pease.

Nocona, after escaping Colonel Ford at Antelope Hills, had retired to bide his time, then strike. The story of his retaliation was told in the ruins of a dozen burned homes on the Pease—and by the fresh-cut scalps that hung on the Comanche lodge poles.

Captain Sul Ross worked fast. He raised his company —sixty hard, two-fisted, straight-shooting veterans of frontier warfare—and set out for Fort Belknap, in Young County eighty miles northwest of Fort Worth. There, he outfitted with government supplies, took on an escort of twenty men from the Second U. S. Cavalry, and marched for the Pease.

This was buffalo country, even on the borders of Fort Belknap, and thus a happy hunting ground for the warriors of the Comanche. Giant herds ranged the grass, and once in a while, in the runs where the shaggy beasts sought water, one could find the tracks of ponies mingled with the hoof marks of the greater animals. The plains scouts knew what this meant, and they were wary as they pushed steadily into the westward landscape.

On December 18, 1860, the sun rose half obscured by one of those frequent sand storms that sweep down over the area, and in mid-morning, as Ross and two Rangers scouted in advance of the main column, the captain suddenly reined in, listened, and held out a hand for silence. Somewhere ahead he had heard the voice of an Indian—singing. They waited atop the little knoll where they had halted and as the wind abated momentarily, and the sand blanket before them thinned, they saw—not two hundred yards before them—the faintly silhouetted outline of a large Comanche village.

And then, in the ranks of the main column, which had slipped up behind the knoll, a horse neighed. The Indian in the village stopped singing, and a death-like quiet settled over the little valley. In it was something ominous, something foreboding. Somewhere out in front an Indian war-whoop split the sand-filled air. Sul Ross knew that the time had come. He didn't hesitate; he attacked.

He shouted an order; and the twenty men of the Second Cavalry swung their charges to the left, to make an encircling ride around the village and cut off possible retreat—for the Rangers had determined this time to rout the Comanche forever, if possible, from the Texas plains. Ross gave the cavalrymen time and then, digging in his spurs and raising a shout that could be heard even by the "long knives" on the opposite side of the village, he charged with his Rangers behind him.

In less time than it takes in the telling they were in among the tipis, hacking, hewing, and using the pistol with deadly, close-range accuracy. The warriors fought with valor, attempting as best they could to hold up the attackers until their women and children could make a get-away on the fleet Indian ponies, many of which already had been nose-looped for a morning buffalo hunt. And in a measure they succeeded. Many of the squaws, and even some of the braves, were fortunate enough to find mounts—but they galloped into the waiting arms of the cavalry dragoons.

The fight was over before it fairly started, having developed rapidly into a sand-wracked game of hide-and-seek, with the Rangers playing hounds to the Comanche hares.

Chief Peta Nocona himself was lucky enough to gain a pony's back and, pulling a fifteen-year-old girl up behind him, he darted northward in an effort to dodge the cavalrymen. Trailing him, on another fast mustang, rode a squaw, an infant in her arms.

But Sul Ross, riding through the tipis, saw him go, and suspecting that the fleeing rider might be the chief, started in hot pursuit, Ranger Lieutenant Tom Kelleher at his side. The two Indian ponies skirted the cavalry escort and made for open country, but the Rangers steadily gained ground. But the Indians, despite their heavily burdened ponies, were giving them a run for it. Nocona rode like a wind-blown devil, both arms of the girl encircling his waist. She was dressed in buckskin shirt and breeches and, though she glanced back every few yards to measure the distance between herself and the pursuers, Ross said later that he believed her to be a boy.

The squaw, clutching the baby to her breast, rode with the buckskin rein free, beating with her heels a steady tattoo on the horse's ribs. A true Centaur of the Plains, this woman of the Comanche, and even Kelleher admired her.

"Take the squaw . . . capture her!" shouted Captain Ross. "I'll go after the chief!"

Ross steadily gained ground, edging ahead of the lieutenant, and, finally, past the fleeing woman. He glanced back only once—to see Kelleher grasp the nose strap of the squaw's pony and pull in the fugitives. Then he turned his sole attention to Peta Nocona.

The chief's horse, weighted as it was, was tiring fast —and now Sul Ross was galloping only twenty yards behind. The captain drew a pistol from his belt, raised it and swung down from the shoulder.

Crack! . . . The girl swayed, clutched once at Nocona's girdle, and toppled from the plunging horse, drilled neatly through the back. But she had caught the girdle, and it was tight about the chieftain's waist; she pulled Nocona with her as she fell.

But Nocona, cat-like, had landed on his feet, and in the flash of a second had whipped the bow from over his shoulders and had strung an arrow with that great speed which only the plains Indian can display. Thus Ross, before he could swerve aside, was made target for two long-shafted arrows, the point of one embedding itself in the left shoulder of his charger.

The captain's horse, stabbed with pain, went wild, but Ross sawed on the bridle, quieted him somewhat and circled back to finish off Nocona. He found the chief standing where he had left him, beside the dying girl, an arrow strung and ready. He loosed it as the Ranger galloped back to renew the attack but the shaft went wide and Ross, clinging to the pommel of his saddle with the left hand, let go another pistol shot. The ball struck Nocona in the right arm, breaking the bone.

"Then," said Captain Ross, telling the story later, "I shot the chief twice through the body, whereupon he deliberately walked to a small tree, and leaning against it, began to sing a wild, weird song."

Ross dismounted and walked toward the chief.

"Surrender?" he called, but Nocona shook his head, brandishing in one last defiant gesture the lance he held in his left hand.

A Mexican member of the Ranger company rode up and dismounted; he carried in the crook of his arm a long-barreled shotgun.

"Finish him!" ordered Captain Ross.

The Mexican raised the shotgun and pulled the trigger.

Nocona, still singing his wild, weird song—the death chant of the Comanche—stood straight as a lance . . . proud . . . erect . . . defiant.

And then he fell—an arrow in the dust.

This is the story—as Sul Ross himself told it in his reports—but in the chapters of history there are contradictory pages. There are those, and the late Colonel

Charles Goodnight is one, who claim that Peta Nocona escaped that slaughter on the Pease and lived to lead his warriors on the raid again. Those historians would have it that it was No-Bah, a sub-chief, who sang the song against the tree and dropped with a load of buckshot in his chest, a claim which was advanced at one time by such a reliable authority as Quanah, son of the chief of chiefs. Be that as it may—

When Captain Ross rode back to the point where Lieutenant Kelleher had ridden down the squaw, he found the officer attempting to allay the woman's fears. Certain that she was marked for death she clutched the baby even more closely to her breast and wept—but not as an Indian woman weeps.

"Look here, Captain," said Kelleher, "this squaw isn't an Indian; she's as white as you are."

"Cynthia Ann Parker," suggested Ross. He called for an interpreter and questioning disclosed that she was indeed the Cynthia Ann Parker who, at the age of nine, had been kidnaped in the raid of 1836 on Silas M. Parker's farm in Limestone County. She had grown up with the wild tribe, married Nocona, and had become the mother of his children—Quanah, Pecos, and little Prairie Flower, the two-year-old baby she carried in her arms in the mad flight from the Rangers.

The Rangers took the back trail to Fort Belknap, exhibiting Cynthia Ann in the scattered settlements through which they passed. Weatherford saw her, and Fort Worth—where the townspeople turned out to look at the "queen" and view with something akin to awe the Indian scalps brought home by the expedition . . .

grim trophies strung on a pole and displayed on Weatherford street.

They took Cynthia Ann to the Parker home near Birdville, and then built her a home in the piney woods of East Texas; but despite her white blood she had become an Indian. Nocona's people were her own, and she grieved for the free life of the plains. The child died first, and then Cynthia Ann.

She could not forget her people; the burning village, shattered like a broken quiver—its arrows in the dust . . .

CHAPTER VIII

A Report to the Adjutant

THE year 1870 . . .

The scene shifters who set the stage of history were busy—placing new back-drops and arranging new settings for the cast made up by the Texas Rangers in the serial drama of a century . . . even a new villain had found a place among the players.

The Sul Ross expedition against Nocona had, for the moment, broken concerted action by the Comanche in the north, but it had not banished the tribesmen from the Texas plains. In spasmodic gestures they made small raids at isolated points extending from the Panhandle to the Gulf, but had failed to muster enough strength to frame a reprisal on the lines of the Great Raid of 1840. But they were taking on new life.

The Ranger force practically had been disbanded after the Civil War—in the belief that the army would protect the frontier—but what did troopers know of savage warfare? The Indians, sensing the situation, were beginning to pull together their shattered remnants. They gathered more strength in the south than elsewhere, and what with Mexican banditti making shoot-and-run raids over the Río Grande, life was none too pleasant . . . and none too safe . . . for the dweller on the border.

Here was the new villain in the piece—the big-hatted, silver-spurred Mexican outlaw who crossed the river

68

to the Texas side, sacked the ranches, and then slithered back to the other side to thumb their noses at the American patrols, who were forbidden by international law from swimming over to settle scores.

Small wonder, then, that Captain H. J. Richarz of the Rangers was nettled. What with the Indians crowding him on one flank and the Mexican banditti on the other, he was having something of a difficult time in making bullets meet.

But allow the Captain to tell his own story—quoted in his own language, and direct from the written report in the files of the Adjutant General at Austin:

Fort Inge, Texas, Dec. 29, 1870.

Colonel James Davidson, Adjutant General, State of Texas:

Sir: Since my last report we have had hard and bloody work here. I will endeavor to make this as short as possible. At daybreak on the fifth of December, I started on a scout with fourteen men and three citizens who had volunteered, to scout the country between the Marcos and the Río Grande, in order to intercept that band of Indians who stole the horses a hundred miles from here, near Fort Inge. That same day I sent messengers from Fort Duncan, who brought in the news that about three hundred Comanches and Kiowas, and about two hundred Kickapoos and Lipans, divided in parties of from fifty to one hundred warriors, all armed with rifles, Spencer rifles and pistols, besides their customary arms, were sweeping this part in every direction. Before I left I had ordered my lieutenant (Haver Weinz) to keep the force held in readiness to mount on half an hour's notice. This party had just come in from a fifteen days' scout to the Devil's River Mountains.

Twenty-five miles from the Río Grande I met a messenger and some United States army officers, who informed me that the scouting party of my company I had mentioned in my last report, under command of Dr. Woodbridge, our medical officer, who had volunteered, and Corporal Eckhart, consisting of fourteen men (one man having been left behind, his horse being lame) on an open prairie, twelve miles from the Río Grande, had overtaken the band of Comanches who had killed David Adams and two Mexicans near Pendencia, had gallantly charged them, and had stood their ground against seventy well-armed savages, and had defeated them, killing eight warriors and wounding about fifteen. I ascertained at the time that this band of Indians, after they were beaten, had retreated toward the Río Grande, and that Dr. Woodbridge's party had buried one of my Rangers, Lorenzo Biediger, who fell in the commencement of the battle, and were camping near the battleground to rest their worn-out horses. So I turned my command towards the lower Chaparoso creek; not finding the trail of the Indians there, I made for the Nueces.

During the night of the eighth of December my guide, whom I had sent towards the Eagle Pass road, to meet a spy, returning to my camp, informed me that another band of Indians had appeared near my post at Fort Inge, in over-whelming numbers; had attacked two of my Rangers at the Blanco, sixteen miles east of Fort Inge, and had killed them. *Their names are Walter Richarz (my son) and Joseph Riff.*

Another band, the Kickapoos, had been seen near Uvalde, riding in the direction of the Frio River. I broke up in the night; arrived before daybreak at the post, and found, to my satisfaction, that Lieutenant Weinz had started with the reserve force in hot pursuit of the murderers of my son and Joseph Riff. Before daybreak the same night, that party who had returned with me had started in a northerly direction, to fall in the trail of the lieutenant, or eventually to intercept the savages on their way to the Canadian River or Indian reserve. With the last three men I had, I intended to start at daybreak the same night towards the Río Grande to assist Dr. Woodbridge's party, as I was informed that old Castro, the chief of the Lipans, had avowed at Piedras Negras that he would revenge his red brethern for the loss inflicted by Dr. Woodbridge's party upon their allies. But I met the Doctor

coming back into the post, who had no loss than the men
above mentioned, and carrying the shield of one of the
Comanche chiefs killed in action as a trophy. The report, as
above stated, is correct in substance. Dr. Woodbridge reports
that he cannot praise enough the bravery and fighting qualities
of my men. Without a moment's hesitation, this little band
had charged seventy well-armed savages (three of my men
were absent on a reconnoitering scout when the fight commenced). The savages had formed two battle lines on a rising
ground, and had soon outflanked my small band. The Indians
fought like demons first; and when an Indian tumbled from
his horse dead or wounded his place was instantly filled with
warriors from out of the second line.

Dr. Woodbridge, stunned by a blow upon his forehead by
an Indian, fell off his horse, but several of my braves, though
fighting themselves against overwhelming numbers, came to
his rescue, and in a second the Doctor had recovered himself
so to join in the work again. His horse was wounded and
lost. The Indians, meanwhile, seeing that they had to deal with
a new sort of combatants, gave up the contest and fell back,
as did my men. They rallied about three hundred yards from
the battleground. I have to mention that, when the action was
in progress, the three men who were on the reconnoitering
tour, drawn by the heavy firing, joined in the attack on the
left flank, killing a chief of the Indians. I hope that this lesson
given to the savages by that heroic little band of Rangers
will do some good; and I am pretty sure that I shall be able
to report another success in a few days.

At the same time, referring to my last report, I would like
to have some reinforcements; at any rate, to be authorized to
fill up my company to the number as organized at first. My
men and horses have not had any rest worth speaking of since
their arrival here. The grass is getting worse every day; and
as the tribes, protected by the Mexicans, have a secure base
of operation of two hundred and fifty miles long, watching
my movements under the eyes of the United States garrison;
having distinctly and formally notified me that they had

determined to drive me from the place, and sweep the country to Béxar County, it is not reasonable to be expected that I can always successfully operate in every direction against half a thousand well-armed savages with thirty-eight privates, not to mention that I am not able to have two strong scouts out in different directions at the same time.

Though we will not count numbers if we fight, I may lose too many men without having the satisfaction to first destroy the enemy. *If it was not for this cursed international law, I know very well what to do to clean out these bloody savages on the other side of the Río Grande.*

I remain, Colonel,

Yours, very respectfully,

H. J. RICHARZ.

Captain commanding Company E, Texas Frontier Force (Official).

Luckily for Captain Richarz and his little band this report never fell into Indian hands. Had the hostiles known their own strength, their own power when massed into a solid unit, they could have swooped down and annihilated the men of Company E with little trouble. But in that day such reports as· these were secret—for the eyes of none but the Adjutant General and his staff at Austin. And so the Indians continued to operate in small bands along the frontier—small bands, but ever growing bolder.

One may assume, from the tone of several paragraphs in Captain Richarz's report, that he wasn't overly enthusiastic about the type of support Uncle Sam's troopers were giving Texas in the matter of Indian warfare. Washington, it appeared, took the attitude that accounts of Indian outrages in Texas were greatly exaggerated—thus the action of the Twelfth Texas

Legislature passing a "joint resolution asking the Congress of the United States to send a joint committee to the frontiers of Texas to inquire into and report upon the number of murders and extent of the outrages committed in Texas during the last five years, and now being committed in Texas, by bands of Indians living within the territory of the United States, and harbored within the Republic of Mexico."

Already a great part of the Comanche and Kiowa tribes had been placed on a reservation near Fort Sill, Indian Territory, but even these warriors were slipping out from under the watchful eyes of the Army to raid into the northern counties of Texas. It was for that reason, perhaps, that the same legislature approved a "joint resolution instructing our Senators and requesting our Representatives in Congress to use their exertions to effect the removal of bands of Comanche and Kiowa Indians to a point at least 150 miles from the civilized settlements or organized counties of Texas."

Already General William Tecumseh Sherman had arrived at Fort Richardson, near Jacksboro, to investigate and report on "the alleged Indian outrages," and on the very night of his arrival, while the general was being wined and dined at the post, a party of Comanches and Kiowa braves (A. W. O. L. from the U. S. reservation at Fort Sill) had raided within a few miles of the post. These Indians, led by three notorious chiefs, Satanta, Satank and Big Tree, had killed seven men on Captain Henry Warren's government wagon train. Thus Sherman got the bloody truth—but more raids were to follow.

And then, money being scarce, a blow fell which laid the Texas frontier open to attack by hostiles all the way from Red River to the border. On May 31, 1871, the seven existing companies of the Texas Rangers were mustered out of service.

"The discharge of the frontier force," explains the adjutant general's report of that year, "was found necessary from its proving too expensive; furthermore, the bonds issued for the frontier expense could not be disposed of nor hypothecated, except at low figures, their value being greatly depreciated by scurrilous and unwarranted attacks made upon them by parties opposing their issuance."

The Indian, in his lodge, heard—and smiled . . .

CHAPTER IX

Lone Wolf Sets a Trap

MAJOR JOHN B. JONES was no chair-warming general.

When he took over command of the Texas Rangers at reorganization of the force under Governor Richard Coke in May of 1874 the dashing little major—whose handlebar whiskers set the fashion of the day—was far better known on the Nueces and on the Pease than in the swivel-chair of the Adjutant's office in Austin.

Restless, ambitious, and with a strict devotion to duty, John Jones wasn't constructed along pacific lines; he had to be in the very thick of things.

Otherwise he might not have made the acquaintance of the notorious Lone Wolf on the Northwest frontier, otherwise old Sam Bass might not have been trapped and shot to death at Round Rock.

Major Jones was always up and at 'em.

But first, a word on the situation which brought on the reorganization of the Rangers. Since that day in May of 1871, when the last of seven companies had been demobilized because of money shortage, conditions on the frontier had gone from bad to worse. The Indian, his most dreaded enemy out of the way, was on the raid again. True, Satanta and Big Tree, the Kiowa chiefs, had been tried at Jacksboro and sentenced to death for the murder of seven wagon train teamsters, but the state, fearing new reprisals from reservation Indians at Fort

Sill, was afraid to hang the culprits; and the Kiowas and Comanches seemed to realize the advantage they held. They took heart, organized new raids.

Local "minute men" companies had been organized in the frontier settlements, but even these had been unable to cope with the situation—the members not having leisure to devote full time to duty—and so, when the Legislature met in May of '74 it considered the matter and forthwith appropriated $75,000 to put the Frontier Battalion into the field again. Consequently, Governor Coke ordered reorganization—the battalion to be made up of six companies of seventy-five men each, to be placed on the frontier from Jacksboro to the Río Grande, and to cover the western interior of the state.

Adjutant General William Steele wanted a good job done and when he looked about for a commander-in-chief to head the new force the first man he thought of was John B. Jones. They put their heads together and wrote certain names on captain's commissions—G. W. Stevens, John Ikard, Jefferson Malty, Rufe Perry, Neal Caldwell and Pat Dolan. And then, when recruiting was completed and the various companies scattered over the west, Major Jones ordered each of his captains to detail him five men for a personal escort—an organization of thirty men to travel with him on tours of inspection from one company to another.

But if the men of this detail had any visions of a "gold brick" job they were soon dispelled . . . for Major Jones' tenure of office became one continual round of "inspections." Major Jones made his headquarters on the front line, wherever it happened to be.

And now—

It is the 12th day of July, 1874, and we find Major Jones and his "inspection" detachment encamped on the lower edge of Lost Valley, a few miles northwest of Jacksboro. Peace lay over the land like a blanket and the Rangers, when they bedded down for the night, slept as soundly as though the dangerous frontier was many miles away. Even the sentry's eyelids drooped during the quiet of the early morning hours.

But dawn had thrown the encampment into a state of intense excitement. A hard-riding horseman had galloped in from Loving's Ranch. He wanted to see the Major. The ranch, he said, had been raided not an hour before, and a war party of a dozen Indians had scampered away with a dozen of the best Loving horses. They had gone off up Lost Valley.

That was all Major Jones wanted to know. He called out an order to his thirty men.

"Saddle and mount!" he shouted. "We'll get these lads before they've gone ten miles."

But the Rangers already were saddling and throwing their equipment together, and scarcely before the messenger from the ranch had recovered his breath, the detachment was on the move. They picked up the trail not far from their own camp—and away they went up the Valley, like ghost riders in the early morning mist. Two miles . . . and Major Jones, riding with a tracker at the head of the column, noticed that the pony tracks seemed fresher, and then—

Whish! A bullet crackled in the air not six inches from the Major's head. It had come from somewhere out front, for the Major noticed a little wisp of smoke and a flash of flame from behind a tree directly ahead of him. He pulled in.

Zip! a slug cut through the column from the left, but sped on to spend itself among the dense foliage bordering the trail on the right. Crack! This time from the right—and then the Major realized what had occurred. He was in a trap; he had ridden in through the mouth of a "horseshoe" and was encircled by he knew not how many savages.

"Dismount and take cover!" he shouted, above the popping of the Kiowa rifles, which now were pouring lead into the Ranger ranks from all sides. He whipped his own rifle from the saddle scabbard, toppled off and took refuge in a gully . . . his Rangers following suit and seeking such protection as the terrain afforded. They were none too soon, for old Lone Wolf, principal chief of the Kiowa who had baited the trap and lain in wait with one hundred and fifty warriors, had ordered the charge.

Down they came—a howling, whooping gang of the most accomplished cut-throats who ever crossed the border on a raid. The situation looked bad, and Major Jones knew it. The savages were well armed and out for scalps, but at the same time the men of his command were jealous of their hair.

The first wave was stopped handily, more than one Kiowa taking the dull plunk of a bullet in the chest as he rushed forward. Ranger Johnny Holmes, a young dandy of delicate appearance and Chesterfieldian manners, got one in the initial sortie, evening scores for the horse that was shot out from under him in the ambush.

After that first attempt Lone Wolf didn't try another charge; he merely contented himself with allowing his men to entrench behind convenient rocks and trees and try to wear down the Rangers with a sniping engagement. An hour passed, and then two hours, the minutes punctuated with sudden bursts of rifle fire. The battle went on—the Rangers firing at gun flashes and wondering what toll they were exacting in the ranks of the enemy.

A Kiowa sniper singled out Ranger W. H. Bailey for his personal attention, zipping over one slug after another at the spot where Bailey was hiding. The bullets came too close, and Bailey shifted his position . . . he died before he had crawled six feet.

Behind another rock Private Lee Corn of Company F lay wounded. Private George Moore of Company E also had stopped a bullet. Twenty-seven men now against one hundred and fifty . . . the situation was desperate. There was, about noon, a lull in the fighting, but it was of short duration. Old Lone Wolf had planned a strategical move. He ordered his braves to let up on the Rangers for the time being and get to work on the Ranger horses with the buffalo guns. No sooner said than done. At least half a dozen of the redskins possessed these long-range weapons, and when they opened up on the trembling horses the Major realized that something must be done, and speedily, if a single man of his command was to get out alive from that trap in Lost Valley.

And then he sensed a companion beside him—Charles Glass of Company B.

"Listen, Major," said Ranger Glass, "I have a plan I think will work and pull us out of this hole. The ammunition has run low and the water supply is out, and we've got to get help. Now here's the plan—my horse is still on his feet, but he may not be long. Let me grab him and make a run for it. . . . He's fast, and I know I can break through and get reinforcements from Jacksboro."

"You can't make it, Glass," said the Major. "They'd get you sure . . . and I won't stand for it."

"But I tell you that I can, sir," persisted Private Glass. "That horse of mine has racing blood in his veins, and if a horse can make it, he can."

The Major flatly refused, but Glass was obstinate.

"All right, then," said the Major, finally. "I'll let you go, but it's against my better judgment. . . . Good luck."

Glass waited only for a slight lull in the fire that was raking the group of horses and then ran for his racer. He swung himself in the saddle, kicked in the spurs, and headed south. But Lone Wolf had seen him mount . . . and sent two braves in pursuit.

Ranger Glass made six hundred yards. A bullet struck the horse and his legs crumpled under him. Glass regained his feet and drew his pistol, but the Kiowa riders were upon him. Glass died . . . sprawled across the body of his racer.

But in the face of this blow the Rangers didn't give ground. They hung on like bulldogs, exchanging shot for shot, until nightfall. For several hours the sniping continued, and then the firing suddenly ceased. The Indians retired—perhaps because the moon happened to be hidden behind the clouds.

In the morning the Rangers took the trail to Jacksboro, to bury their dead and dress their wounds. Tersely, Major Jones reported to the Adjutant General at Austin that, in addition to his own casualties of two dead and three wounded, his detachment had lost "twelve horses killed and permanently disabled; had killed three Indians and wounded three; captured one horse, blankets, bows, arrows, etc., etc."

"Etc., etc."—well-used terms in the reports that early-day Rangers made to the Adjutant's office.

Major Jones ever was a man of few words, and those very briefly spoken—or written. His reports, that he made as his "headquarters" moved up and down the frontier, bear witness to that. For instance, his remarks on the colorful Sam Bass affair cover but a few paragraphs, but the report of the Adjutant General made to Governor R. B. Hubbard under the date of December 2, 1878, has this to say about the Major:

"During the past spring, when four railroad trains were robbed in quick succession near Dallas, urgent appeals were made from that city, and from railway and express companies for assistance; in answer to which a small detachment of the Frontier Battalion, acting under immediate command of Major John B. Jones, succeeded in killing or capturing nearly all of the parties concerned in the robberies.

"It is due to Major Jones to say that he obtained the first clue to the robberies, and followed it up until the killing of the leader, F. S. Bass, at Round Rock, Texas. During the period in which the hunt was going on he was often frustrated by the ill-timed haste of private detectives and others anxious to get the rewards."

Major Jones commanded the Rangers for many years and saw a variety of action in Texas that few men have experienced, but the trap he set for the notorious Sam Bass was one of the greater highlights of his career.

Early in the year 1878 the Major, through some source known only to himself, had discovered the Bass gang's hangout near Denton, in the north of Texas, and he sent several Rangers, with Captain June Peak in command, to scout about the city incognito and learn what they could about the movements of the train-robbing terrors.

Peak was so successful that he made contact with one of the outlaws, Jim Murphy, and, presumably at the behest of the Major, the Captain offered Murphy immunity if he would lead his chief into a trap. O. M. Roberts, governor at that time, had promised after a conference with Jones, to be lenient with Murphy if he agreed to work.

In July Sinful Sam and his merry boys left Denton for Waco and on the way south Sam, hearing there was gold to be had in the safe of Storekeeper P. G. Peters of Round Rock, planned a raid. The band started—reached Belton. There, Murphy dropped a card in the post informing Major Jones, who was waiting at Austin, of the scheduled time for the robbery.

Jones acted at once. He sent Sergeant Dick Ware,

Sergeant C. L. Neville and Ranger George Herald on the road to Round Rock.

On the 21st of July Sinful Sam and four of his gang, Seba Barnes, Murphy, Jackson and Underwood, appeared on the streets of the town. They walked into Peters' store. Deputy Sheriffs Hige Grimes and Maurice Moore followed. They found the outlaws casually surveying the stock of the store. Deputy Grimes walked directly up to Sam Bass.

"I want to see if you are armed," said Grimes. "Do you have a six-shooter?"

"Two of them," said Sam Bass, as calmly as a man in church, "and here they are."

He drew—shot Grimes dead and seriously wounded Moore.

The Rangers, waiting in a near-by barn, heard the firing and rushed to the scene. The bandits were leaving the store. Herald shot Seba Barnes through the head. Ward cracked down on Bass and wounded the bandit, but he managed to mount a horse and gallop away. Sergeant Neville took up the trail, however, and two miles from the town found the robber chief lying under a tree in a dying condition. Jackson and Underwood had deserted him.

Sam Bass robbed no more trains in Texas . . . the Major's trap had been too tight.

Major Jones, who died in Austin several years ago, was quiet, but he was dangerous; always at the front, his headquarters where the line happened to be—one of the bravest and the most gallant of the gentlemen who wore the big white hats.

"For no man could beat him to a real live scrap with the enemy," says one of the last surviving captains of the Rangers. "He was a man . . . John Jones."

—But so was Captain Roberts, who took his orders . . .

John B. Jones, Major of the Frontier Battalion. *Photo courtesy of the Texas Ranger Hall of Fame and Museum, Waco, Texas.*

CHAPTER X

Dan W. Roberts . . . Captain Courageous

HOLD your fire until you're certain, aim true, and then let go . . . do that, and you can't be far wrong, in the estimation of Captain Dan W. Roberts, oldest living Texas Ranger and one of the last survivors of the famous Frontier Battalion that chased the Indian from the banks of the San Saba and helped bring peace to the long miles of the Texas badlands.

And the Winchester rifle, if you want the captain's word for it, is about the best implement ever invented for the purpose of cultivating the soil of a new country —it's one reason, says he, that we are able to enjoy today the comforts of a "patent leather civilization."

And Captain Roberts of Austin, out of the wisdom of his ninety-three years, should know . . . for John B. Jones was once his major.

It was, after all, only natural that Dan Roberts should become a Ranger and an Indian fighter, for the business was in his blood. For his father, Alexander Roberts, had fought in the battle of Plum Creek, the fight that shattered the Great Comanche Raid of 1840 . . . and then, too, young Daniel had been brought up on the lore of a frontier country. After Plum Creek the Roberts family moved back to their home state, Mississippi, and there, on October 10, 1841, Dan was born; the family moving back to Texas when he was two years old.

"And so," says the captain, "I was reared, and almost rocked, in the cradle of Texas warfare."

He was, however, thirty-two years old when he met the Indians for the first time in actual combat—in the Deer Creek fight near Round Mountain about sixty miles south of Austin, in August of '73; an event largely responsible for the Ranger's commission Roberts received the following year.

Mr. and Mrs. Thomas Phelps, who lived in Blanco County south of Round Mountain, had been scalped by a band of Comanches and the citizens of the community had mustered for mutual protection, the rally taking place at the Roberts home. The general situation was discussed and it was decided that the next time the Indians came plundering into that section they would meet unexpected opposition. And they did. When the redskins came back, a few weeks later, the vigilantes were ready and waiting. Following on a fresh trail the whites caught up to the enemy after a fifteen-mile chase —and the battle of Deer Creek was on, ten Texans against twenty-seven Comanches.

The Indians had led their pursuers into a valley, waited on the ridges above, and had opened fire as the Texans rode in. More or less trapped, the latter dismounted, sought shelter behind trees, and returned the leaden compliment.

Dan Roberts was to fight fiercer battles in his day, but that hour's sniping engagement on Deer Creek— during which he used an old Spencer saddle gun to good advantage—came near being not only his first but his last . . . for when the scrape was over he was bleeding so severely from a bullet hole through the left thigh that the wound was believed, at first, to be mortal. Two others had been nicked—Dan's brother George, with a wound on the face; and Joe Bird, whose shoulder had been grazed by a slug. The Indians made four graves.

A small battle, compared to some of those fought on the frontier, but a spectacular one—at least spectacular enough to attract the attention of the current Legislature, which voted to present Roberts with a repeating model Winchester rifle. Incidentally, he still has the weapon.

About the first of May in the following year Roberts, having recovered from his wound, informed his neighbors that he was going into New Mexico to see what that country offered the settler; but even while he packed supplies there came a letter from Captain Rufe Perry in Austin, one of the men Major John B. Jones had selected to lead a company of the reorganized Frontier Battalion.

"Meet me in Austin May 10," Captain Perry had written. That was all, except the signature—and so May 10 found Roberts walking up Congress avenue in the capital city; and as chance would have it he met Perry on the avenue two blocks from the capitol building.

"Here's something for you," said the captain, after a word of greeting. He handed over a rolled document and the man from Deer Creek unfolded it—a lieutenant's commission in the Texas Rangers, the ink of Governor Richard Coke's signature hardly dry.

"I guess you've got me," said Roberts, folding the paper and stowing it in his pocket.

August on the San Saba . . . Captain Perry's Company D was encamped in Menard County, near the army post of Fort McKavett. Lieutenant Roberts was scouting the Little Saline and the prairies to the westward. Once or twice his detachment had jumped small bands of Comanches but had not come close enough for effective combat. Life was easy on the San Saba . . . and the Lieutenant drew his hundred dollars.

November . . . and Major Jones had come to camp on one of his "inspection" tours; and it seemed that where the Major went trouble always trailed behind. Fresh from the Lone Wolf fight in Lost Valley, he had ridden in on the 20th with thirty men, Lieutenant B. F. Best the second in command. And, as might be expected, things began to occur within twelve hours . . . for the very morning after the escort's arrival two Rangers, sent by Captain Perry up Elm Creek to get a supply of beef, came riding in with the news that they had been attacked by Indians a few miles to the westward.

The horses of half the headquarters escort already were saddled at the time, a scout having been scheduled, and so the detachment took the trail immediately under the command of Lieutenant Best, leaving the men of Company D to follow as soon as possible. Roberts ordered a detail of the company to saddle and within twenty minutes they were trailing in the wake of the escort, catching up near Saline Creek, eight miles away. The two detachments merged, struck a gallop on the fresh

Indian trail, and overhauled the enemy within four miles.

"They were riding easily, and saw us about the time we sighted them," said Roberts, recalling the incident, "but they did not attempt to run, and I knew we were in for a fight. I told the men in my group to aim low in order to kill horses if they missed Indians."

The Rangers rode down to the attack, holding their fire until they were within easy pistol shot, and then the chief of the Indians, who had been riding at the rear of his column, spurred to the front and wheeled his men about, bringing them into an open order skirmish line.

"As pretty a military movement as I ever saw," said Roberts, who followed suit by breaking his column and spacing his Rangers at proper intervals. The respective moves placed the chief at the right of his braves, and the Lieutenant at the left of his line, so that they were facing each other across a narrow strip of "no-man's land."

The Indians, a large war party, opened fire, but still the Rangers waited. The firing stopped and then the chief, kicking his heels into his horse, advanced a few yards across the front toward Roberts—who called the bluff, riding out an equal distance to meet the Indian. They hesitated for a moment and then the chief raised his rifle, an improved Winchester, and let go. Wham! Lieutenant Roberts heard the thud of the bullet as it struck his horse in the shoulder and, fearing that the animal might fall, jumped clear and pulled up his own rifle. A great game followed.

"The chief tried a war dance on me to draw my

fire," recalls Roberts, "but it didn't succeed . . . I held my Winchester on him, hoping he would settle down so I couldn't miss. But to make matters worse, another Indian had found my range and was whanging over lead uncomfortably close."

And then the chief, tiring of his dance, settled down, just as Roberts had hoped he would. Lieutenant Dan pulled the trigger. The Comanche . . . "settled down." Meanwhile, Corporal Thurlow Weed who had ridden up to aid his officer, had spotted the dangerous sniper. Weed dismounted, dropped on one knee, took steady aim, and let go . . . the sniper yelled, sprang into the air, fell face down.

The Rangers charged.

Lieutenant Roberts' horse was wounded, but not seriously enough to keep him out of the chase, and away went Roberts, Private George Bryant galloping at his side. They singled out two Indians riding one horse and, after a hot chase of half a mile, drew up within range. Bryant then checked his mount, raised his rifle, and fired from the saddle, the bullet taking the rear rider in the back of the head. The other rider, now alone, plunged on, the Lieutenant behind him; but the Indian, knowing that his pony was failing, jumped off and raised his hands in sign of surrender.

"I had sworn not to take prisoners," said Roberts, "but the sight of this fellow, begging for his life, weakened me. I held him until some of my men rode up, then turned him over to Weed, who took him back to camp, leaving me to resume the chase."

Thus Little Bull of the Comanches, one of the few

hostiles ever taken prisoner by the Rangers, was started on his way to the penitentiary at Huntsville, where he died a prisoner of war.

For two miles Roberts' men and the escort detachment kept up a running fight with the fleeing tribesmen, killing five on the field and capturing a supply of arms. For the finale of the story glance at the Adjutant General's report for that year:

"Lieutenant Roberts gave up the pursuit on account of the horses of his command being broken down, but Lieutenant L. P. Beavert, Company B, Frontier Battalion, with a detachment of Major Jones' escort, kept up the pursuit, and with only two men (the horses of the others having also broken down) overtook the five remaining Indians when they took refuge in a cave among the rocks, where he fought them until night, killing one and wounding one. Lieutenant Beavert remained at the cave, endeavoring to keep them there until daylight, but under cover of the intense darkness, the Indians crawled out and made their escape."

After the fight the captured brave, Little Bull, was placed on a pack mule and with his feet tied under the animal's belly, sent away to Austin—as a present to Governor Coke. His Excellency, having no use for him, sent him to Huntsville.

Late in '74, at the resignation of Perry, the captain's commission went to Lieutenant Roberts—an event that marked the beginning of four years of active service for one of the most gallant of the state's "captains courageous."

August found him and his Company D swapping

blows with the Indians on the Staked Plains, trailing Chief Magoosh's Lipans into the hills of the Concho; meeting them in hit-and-go combats, both sides retiring to strike again. And in one of the skirmishes on the Staked Plains two Comapny D men, J. B. Gillette and Ed Seiker, captured a white man and a Mexican who had been taken prisoners as boys and brought up in the cult of the Lipan warrior. Fisher, the white man, who had been too long with the tribe to revert back to the ways of his own people, escaped and was found years later living among the reservation Indians at Fort Sill.

In that same year, 1875, Captain Roberts appeared in Colorado City—under orders from the Adjutant General to investigate the conduct of a company commanded by the one-armed Ranger, Captain Marsh. Marsh had heard one Mr. Patterson "cussing" the Rangers and, despite the absence of an arm lost in the service of the Confederacy, had waded in to do fistic battle. The man won, and in celebrating the victory, raised a rather full-bodied disturbance. The Rangers warned him, then killed him. Citizens asked an investigation, and that was Captain Roberts' job. His report exonerated his fellow officer.

September of 1875 . . . and the Mason County cattle war. Cattle thievery had been rampant; bad blood had arisen between the ranchers and the German settlers of Mason City; and the former had come down on the town "to burn up the Dutch." The feud already had cost fifteen lives before Captain Roberts arrived with the Rangers. Twenty-two arrests were made; order was restored in Mason County.

The Plains again . . . and then, in '78, the Mexican Border, where the captain got a first-hand view of the new menace that was challenging the supremacy of the Texas Rangers. Roberts resigned in '82 and went to New Mexico for the betterment of his wife's health.

But once a Ranger, always a Ranger—at least in spirit. Captain Roberts came back, and although he never again entered the service, he is just as much a Ranger today as he was in the days when he chased the redskins on the San Saba.

He is nearing ninety-three, and although his sight and his hearing is not what it one time was, he likes nothing better than to sit in his home on Elmwood street in Austin and look back over the bold days of the past.

He is willing — now — to forgive his Comanche enemies on the ground that they believed that they were being ousted from a country they considered their own. But in this case, says the Captain, the red man's claim was not good—for Texas had belonged to Mexico.

He is willing, too, to shake the hand of Uncle Sam, having been one of those who believed that the army failed to co-operate as it might have in the suppression of the Indian. Uncle Sam is quite all right, says the captain, but—

"His striped breeches did sag on us sometimes when we needed help."

And Mrs. Roberts, white-haired and charming, nods her approval. She ought to know—for she spent six years in a Ranger camp on the fringe of the wild frontier.

Company D., Texas Rangers, 1888.   *Photo courtesy of the Texas Ranger Hall of Fame and Museum, Waco, Texas.*

CHAPTER XI

The Battalion Rides

It wasn't all romance—the work of the Texas Ranger.

It wasn't all battles, and adventure and the thrills of a pulse-quickening chase, with Death hanging to the saddle strings and Life beckoning over the horizon.

It was work—tough, heart-breaking work, with a dozen false trails followed to every one with adventure at the end. Hard days in the saddle, long hours across the desert without water and without food—and then, perhaps, the salvation of an alkali pool and a chunk of beef, unseasoned, and half raw.

These men rode . . .

And they didn't call it romance; the Ranger private in the ranks earned every penny of the forty dollars a month that the state paid him four times a year.

If you doubt it glance over the report of John B. Jones, major commanding the Frontier Battalion (five companies of thirty-two men each) covering the period from September 1, 1875, to August 31, 1876.

The files on the Rangers preceding his day, were destroyed in a fire at the Adjutant General's office in 1855, but the official communications on the activities of the following organizations furnish some insight into the hardships encountered by the Gentlemen in the White Hats—though even these should be multiplied somewhat in the case of those who rode the earlier trails.

The Major's report, in part:

COMPANY F, FRONTIER BATTALION

September, 1875—Company reorganized under Lieut. Neal Caldwell. Lieut. Caldwell resigned August 31, 1876. Company started on a scout to Pecos River.

October, 1875—Returned on the 18th. Found no Indians, but picked up three horses at a deserted Indian camp. Returned horses to owners. Four hundred and twenty-eight miles traveled on this scout.

November, 1875—On 13th, Lieut. Caldwell and twelve men left in pursuit of party of nine Indians and seven horses seen passing out toward Devil's River the evening before. Found no trail.

January, 1876—Under orders from Adjutant General company reached Live Oak County to quell disturbances in that county. On 11th arrested three men charged with murder. On December 14th, at Dogtown, took charge of three prisoners charged with horse stealing; turned them over to civil authorities; same day arrested another man.

February, 1876—On 11th, Sergeant Witt and nine men went in pursuit of a cattle herd to recover some stolen horses. Found that horses had been returned to owners. On 20th, K. Hunt, murderer of Bill Piper in Williamson County, arrested.

April, 1876—On 11th, Sergt. Witt and nine men found trail of Indians on main Frio, where it was reported a man's horse had been shot from under him and a boy killed. Lost trail on 13th. Mr. Williams and a boy reported killed on the Nueces this month. On 21st, Sergeant Witt arrested Frank Lottee, charged with the theft of hogs. On 21st, Lieutenant Caldwell and fifteen men learned at Point Rock that Indians had stolen horses on the 19th and had wounded one man. Got on trail and followed it in direction of Devil's River, across the plains, a distance of seventy miles, without any water. Horses beginning to fall and men suffering, quit the trail at 2:30 p. m. on 23rd. Struck southwest and reached water on

Devil's River at 8 o'clock on 24th. Command had been without water for forty-six hours. Found a large Indian trail going northwest just before reaching water; about two days old, with eighty or ninety horses and mules. Detachment too weak to follow.

May, 1876—On 9th, Sergeant Witt with eleven men learned that —— Nexon had been killed by Indians on the head of Camp Wood Creek on 2nd, and that several horses had been stolen on the Frio on 3rd. Found no trail. On 17th, Sergeant Jones arrested Alex Gregory, charged with assault to murder. Turned him over to sheriff of Kerr County. On 21st, Sergeant Witt and nine men reported for duty to Sheriff Bonnett of Béxar County to guard public funds being carried to Austin.

June, 1876—On 23rd, started on scout with Major Jones.

August, 1876—On 4th, Sergeant Witt and thirteen men left on scout and learned that, on 1st, seven Indians went from Nueces to Frio and stole thirty-five horses from Frio Canon. Found no trail.

Four thousand, two hundred and seventy-one miles traveled by company in weekly scouts and patrols, which were regularly kept up.

COMPANY E, FRONTIER BATTALION

September, 1875—Company reorganized under Lieut. B. S. Foster.

April, 1876—On 9th, Sergeant Israel arrested C. King for stealing steers and turned him over to civil authorities.

June, 1876—On 1st, two detachments, one under Lieutenant Foster and ten men, and one under Sergeant Williams with ten men, in search of herd of stolen cattle in Burnet County.

July, 1876—On 11th, Lieutenant Foster and ten men struck an Indian trail on Colorado River and followed it thirty-five miles; discovered the Indians at 4 a. m.; charged their camp; routed them; wounded one Indian and captured forty horses. As force was too small to fight the Indians and hold the horses, retired. They had eleven lodges and there were fifty

Indians. Captured new blankets marked U. S. I. D., calico, mosquito bars, saddles, crockery, utensils, etc., proving that the Indians were lately from some reservation. On 25th, company started on scout under Major Jones and Company A, passing over ground of late fight.

Eleven thousand, three hundred and fifty-nine miles were traveled by the daily patrols, regular weekly scouts and detachments of company during the year.

COMPANY A, FRONTIER BATTALION

September, 1875—On 1st, company reorganized under Lieut. Ira Long. On 27th, joined Major Jones from Wise County. During rest of month company engaged assisting Major Jones and civil authorities of Mason County in quelling disturbances.

October, 1875—On 10th, Lieutenant Long and detachment arrested and captured a party against whom he had warrants.

November, 1875—On 3rd, six men of company, with Sheriff Beard, captured some cattle thieves. Still on duty in Mason County.

December, 1875—Still on duty in Mason County. Arrested George Childers on suspicion of being Bill McIver of Madison County. Released for want of evidence to hold him.

January, 1876—Still on duty in Mason County.

February, 1876—From 1st to 8th, on duty in Burnet County, with Judge Turner holding district court.

March, 1876—On 1st, Corporal Nelson and four men assisted Sheriff Beard in arresting a party under indictment.

April, 1876—On 11th, company on escort to major commanding, visiting Companies D, B and E near Round Timbers on Brazos.

May, 1876—From 1st to 10th, encamped at New Albany, Shackelford County. On 19th, escort of major commanding, visited Companies D and E and reached Company F on 31st.

June, 1876—From 5th to 10th, on duty with Company F. On 23rd, company started scout to Devil's and Pecos Rivers.

July, 1876—Returned from above scout and started on a new one on 25th.

August, 1876—Still on same scout. On 1st, near source of Colorado, at head of Champion Creek, struck eleven Indian wigwams, very recently abandoned. Blankets, tent covers, saddles, trinkets, etc., were found. Six miles above twelve more wigwams were found abandoned, about the same time. March stopped by prairie having been fired. On 2nd, Priv. W. P. Gaynor was accidentally shot in the hand whilst on guard.

Four thousand and forty miles were traveled by company during the year.

EL PASO COUNTY FRONTIERSMEN

November, 1875—Under command of Lieut. Telesfero Montes, company followed trail of three Indians, who stole nine horses and one mule from Socorro. Killed one Indian, recovered seven horses and mules and captured three Indian ponies.

March, 1876—Reports Indians coming in often; were in twice last week; stole horses.

April, 1876—On 16th, Indians stole horses from near San Elizario. Followed trail for two days and nights. Saw them go over the mountains into their reservation at Dog Canon. While watering the horses and resting, company fired into by about two hundred Indians, armed with needle guns and pistols. Was obliged to retreat, taking advantage of night.

* * *

There were other companies in the field, of course, but the foregoing reports are sufficient to show the wide variety of duties the Ranger was called upon to perform. During one year alone the "flying squadron" headquarters company of Major Jones went from one end of the line to the other eight times, traveling 3,200 miles.

And the commander of the Frontier Battalion in those

days had worries other than long horseback rides, sniping engagements and detail paper work. For example, this excerpt from another of the Major's reports to the Adjutant:

"The Quartermaster found much difficulty at first in procuring supplies for the command at reasonable prices. Parties furnishing supplies to organizations of the kind heretofore have invariably charged exorbitant prices for everything; in some instances, as much as seventy-five cents per pound for coffee, $15 per hundred for flour, ten cents per pound for beef, and other things at like exorbitant rate. But, by judicious management and by having the *money* to pay for what he wanted, he has succeeded in purchasing at reasonable rates; never has paid more than thirty-three cents for coffee, $6.50 for flour, and four and a half cents for beef. He is now having coffee delivered to the companies in the field at twenty-six cents, flour at five and beef at from two to three and a half cents a pound. So much for having the money to pay for what we purchase . . ."

But with the companies in the field food sometimes could not be had at any price. In the yellow files of the old Dublin Telephone may be found the following narrative by Ranger J. M. R. Stephen describing his bitter experiences on an Indian scout in Erath County:

"In the latter part of February, 1860, while a Texas Ranger, twelve of us left our camp one morning for a ten-day scout. We traveled north to near Hubbard Creek, where we camped for the night. Next morning we thought best to travel up the creek to its head. About 10 o'clock we came to a trail of Indians that crossed the creek, and as best we could count, were driving twenty-five or thirty head of horses, the sign indicating that they had passed the day before. We followed this trail about five miles when we found where they had camped the night before.

"We stopped and ate our dinners and grazed our horses on some wild rye for some two hours, then took the trail again, following it until almost night. The buffaloes were very plentiful and we found the carcasses of two that the Indians had killed. About the time we went into camp for the night a drove of buffalo came near and we killed a nice fat calf, which we enjoyed for supper.

"The next morning we took the trail and followed it about ten miles, when the buffalo became so plentiful that they made it very difficult to keep the trail; in fact, we lost it, but traveled the course the trail was going in hopes of picking it up again, but never succeeded. We came at last to the head of a considerable creek and in looking about for the trail we found the legs of a man. We hunted around and found nearly all the remaining portions of the body. From all appearances he had been killed, or had died, six or eight months previously. We found his hat and part of his clothing, gathered them up and piled them in a small washout and covered them with some thin flat rocks that we got out of the creek. We threw dirt over the crude grave so as to cover the corpse two or three inches deep. We named the stream Dead Man's Creek, and it goes by that name to this day.

"As to how this man met his fate I am not able to say, but we were of the opinion that he was a regular soldier and had deserted from a government post and had been slain by Indians, or had starved or frozen to death.

"The skies clouded that evening and in the morning

there was a threat of rain, so we made for what we took to be the Double Mountain Fork of the Brazos River. On account of continued cloudy, wet weather our provisions gave out and our horses were all ridden down, so we camped at first one place and the other, so as to give our horses a chance to get something to eat for several days.

"To add to our troubles I was taken with a violent cold. My head ached for three days and nights without ceasing, and I began to think there was going to be a funeral occasion. I banked my feet at the fire until I burned off all the front of my pants from the knees down. We were camped on the side of a mountain and it was cold enough for January. As soon as the weather moderated we started out in the same direction and, after traveling most of the day, killed a small, poor deer and ate it.

"We came to a canyon and traveled up it some distance, and discovered the first and last Indians we saw on this scout. They yelled and waved their bows and motioned for us to come over. We shot four or five times at them but to no avail, the distance being too great. Finally two of them got off their horses to bellow and paw up the dirt like bulls; and after so long a time they got on their horses and galloped over the hill away from us. We watched them as long as we could see them and then started on the march to some mountains in hope of finding buffalo or other game, as we were out of rations.

"We made it to the mountains but failed to find anything in the way of a bird or animal. We had eaten only a few mouthfuls of poor venison that morning and we were all very hungry. It was a cold, damp night and we rested as best we could until morning, when we saddled our horses and started out, still hoping to find buffalo, deer or something we could eat. But it seemed that fate was against us, as we traveled all day without sighting any game except a small bunch of antelope. We tried to get one, but in vain, and all we had to eat during the day was four or five spring frogs, which we broiled and divided.

"Night came on again with nothing to eat. We were almost starved, and John Salmon, who was in command of the scouts, said we would stand the hunger one more day and then, if we could not find something, would kill one of the horses. I was so weak I was almost ready to give up. My horse was the one to be butchered, as he was in fairly good fix, but was lame in one of his feet.

"As luck would have it, we came in sight of four head of cattle that the Indians had driven away, and we succeeded in killing one. Of all the eating, we did it that evening and night! No salt or bread, but I can say truthfully, I ate as much as fifteen pounds before I was satisfied; and Salmon said he ate as much, if not more. Strange to say, not one felt any inconvenience from the feast.

"We stopped at that camp five days and four nights. We killed a bear and had plenty of fat beef and turkey. Our horses rested and got all the wild rye they could eat. We finally made it back to our camp at Ranger after thirty-one days absence. Our comrades had given us up for lost."

It wasn't all fun and romance—this rubbing down

the rough spots of a wild country. But the Frontier Battalion was doing its work well, so well that the Indian, worn and weary from unceasing warfare, was giving up the struggle, accepting the bitterness of defeat, and returning to the reservations. Soon the Battalion would be needed no longer on the West Texas frontier— but matters were different on the Mexican border.

Silver spurs jangled on the Río Grande—the big-hatted banditti, growing more arrogant day by day, were on the raid.

Captain Leander H. McNelly

CHAPTER XII

Don Juan Cortina Harries the Border

HIS Excellency Señor Don Juan Cortina, general of the Mexican army and Lord Mayor of Matamoras, liked beefsteak—especially if it was on the hoof and had a Texas flavor . . . and since a great man's tastes usually are copied by his admirers, even in the matter of sirloins, so did Don Juan's troopers.

They all liked beefsteak—and since El General Cortina always held with Napoleon that an army travels best on its stomach, and since there were fat steers to be had on the Texas side of the Río Grande, things had been happening down in that corner of the world.

In true fact, Don Juan, figuratively and literally, had been raising proverbial "hell on the border."

Of course His Excellency, smiling his suave, white-toothed smile, denied it all. What! He . . . Juan Nepucenemo Cortina, mayor of a city, general of an army . . . a common cattle thief! A ladrone! Caramba! What fools, these Texans!

But the border Texans had their own ideas about cattle lifters, and their private opinions on the subject of Don Juan Cortina. They knew him only too well—perhaps better than Cortina himself realized. They remembered when, in '59 he had entered Brownsville at the head of a party of armed Mexicans and had committed murders and other outrages. They had seen, in succeeding years, too many burned ranches; too many depleted herds; too many skinned steers; too many altered brands among the cattle of the Mexican ranches across the border. These Texans knew where the stock was going. If Cortina's brigade wasn't getting both beef and hides . . . then who was?

And that wasn't all—not by any means. The American ranchers had positive and indisputable proof that Cortina held, and was executing, a contract with Cuba to supply that country with a shipload of beef cattle every week; and these steers, loaded out of Bagdad, carried the brands of Texas owners.

The ranchers on the northern bank of the Río Grande were mad . . . good and mad. This thing had been taking place for too many years, and the border area was no longer a safe place in which to live. They had complained to Austin until they were sick and weary of the job, and as time rocked on, with conditions growing steadily worse, they became desperate—sleeping with six-shooters under the pillows and rifles within easy reach, for no man knew when the banditti would single out his own particular herd.

True, Governor E. J. Davis, the "carpet-bagger," had succeeded, with bitter opposition from East Texas, in putting through the Legislature in 1870 a bill providing for a Frontier Battalion to cope with the particular situation, and the company, in command of Captain L. H. McNelly, was working on the border—but even these brave and fearless men had been hampered in their work by a multiple of restrictions. For one thing, they received no support from the federal military, both the Rangers and the troops being forbidden by international law from crossing the Río Grande to chase the rading banditti.

Captain McNelly was doing all he could—but thirty-odd men against an army brigade of brigands aren't many.

The ranchers complained again to Austin, this time more bitterly than ever—and July of 1875 found Adjutant General William Steele on the border investigating. Among other observations he reported the following to Governor Richard Coke:

". . . that parties have been and still are being organized on Mexican soil for the purposes of plundering ranches, stores and individuals, and other parties, for the purpose of collecting herds of cattle in Texas and driving them into Mexico for sale. That these acts are committed with the knowledge and connivance of Mexican officials.

". . . that parties of Americans living near the Nueces have banded together with the object of stopping the killing of cattle for their hides, but have themselves committed the greater crimes of murder and arson.

". . . that many merchants in Corpus Christi and elsewhere have aided and abetted the hide peeling by buying the stolen hides knowingly.

". . . that the negro U. S. soldiery give no sense of security to citizens outside of towns, but on the contrary are regarded with fear.

". . . that the country near the Río Grande is being rapidly depopulated of good citizens on account of the insecurity of life and property."

The Adjutant enclosed affidavits.

Lawrence J. Hynes, of Santa Maria Ranch in Cameron County, had this to say: "A sense of insecurity prevails among the residents who have anything to lose, and their only concern is to save their lives . . ."

Arthur J. Erwin of Brownsville gave this testimony: "I commenced with eleven hundred head of cattle; I have on hand about two hundred head; I have sold about two hundred head. The balance have been robbed from me by bands of armed Mexicans . . . I am now in Brownsville, where I shall stay until I can return to my ranch with safety . . ."

Thaddeus M. Rhodes of Relampago ranch was bitter: "I was robbed by Juan N. Cortina and his band of cut-throat invaders; my houses and fences were burned."

Nicholas Champion, who had one thousand cattle in '61, swore: "I now have about fifty head."

There were many, many others. Even the prosperous Mexican ranchers on the American side were not safe.

Jesus Sandoval, whose life was threatened and whose rancho was fired, said this in his affidavit: "I know from men of undoubted veracity that Juan Cortina has many cattle on his ranches which were stolen in Texas and have yet the brands of the rightful owners . . ."

Anastasio Cavasos: "More than eight hundred head of my cattle have been stolen from me and carried into Mexico . . ."

But one of the most damning of all the affidavits was one from Sergeant George A. Hall, spy for McNelly's company of Texas Rangers:

"I was directed by Captain McNelly to proceed to Bagdad, Mexico, and ascertain all I could in relation to cattle driven to that place by General Cortina of the Mexican army, to be shipped to Havana by a Spaniard named Bustamente. I arrived at Bagdad on the seventh instant (June, 1875). I saw cattle just above the town, and was informed that there were four hundred and eighty of them. I examined the brands as carefully as I could under the circumstances, knowing that I was suspected and closely watched by the Mexicans in charge. They had heard I was a detective, and I had to make them believe to the contrary.

"I saw a large number of beeves with American brands. I copied about sixteen brands. One of them is the brand of Hale and Parker; another Rabb's. I saw a brand which I believe was I-K, one of Captain Richard King's of Santa Gertrudes ranch. Some of the brands had been freshly burned. The men assisting to ship the cattle told me they were satisfied they were mostly from Texas.

"I have the copies of the brands yet in my possession and will submit them to some person well acquainted with the brands in this section and he can designate the owners. *I believe nearly all the brands were American, or those of residents of Texas.* I saw a large pile of beef hides, and I saw American brands on them. I think there were five hundred of them. I saw a large pile of dried beef, done up in bales or packages. *I believe there was* 100,000 *pounds of it.*

"I went on board the steamship and saw some of the cattle shipped, and a considerable quantity of dried beef.

"Señor Bustamente pays Captain Moore of the Eunice Huston forty dollars a day for lightering. He pays the steamer Jessie one hundred dollars per trip for towing Captain Moore's vessel. Bustamente offered Captain Moore fifty dollars a day to remain at Bagdad until the steamer returns for another cargo. The steamship is lying about three miles from Bagdad.

"I was told that Señor Bustamente is paying hands from two to five dollars a day to assist in loading the steamship.

"I was informed that General Cortina had been at Bagdad several days, and left the same evening I arrived at Clarksville—the sixth instant. He had seventy-five men with him. *I was told that at least half the horses his men were riding had American brands.*

(Signed) G. A. HALL."

So much for the case against Señor Don Juan Cortina —who liked the Texas beefsteak, unwisely and too well. He had, indeed, raised the proverbial "hell on the border" and yet he smiled his suave, bland smile. And something had to be done about it—but what?

The United States troops couldn't—and wouldn't— cross the border in pursuit of thieves. Secretary of War Belknap was somewhat rabid on that subject . . . international law and all that sort of thing. He had given strict orders in that respect, and he wanted them observed.

The State of Texas was financially unable to raise, at that time, additional companies of the Frontier Battalion. But that didn't prevent Adjutant General Steele from dispatching these suggestions to Governor Coke at Austin:

"The first necessity is that the despotic power of Cortina be removed. Second, that there must be such an agreement between officers of the peace on both sides, as will prevent the collection of criminals on the line, where they can escape from one nationality to the other, as may be necessary to their safety.

"Failing in such peaceable measures, it is necessary that there should be a large force, under one head, on the Río Grande, *with orders to pursue and capture felons into Mexico, if necessary.* The immunity from pursuit no longer existing, stealing would be reduced to the petty proportions that is found everywhere."

And that was all L. H. McNelly, captain of Texas Rangers, wanted to hear.

He had sweated long enough.

General Juan Cortina. *Photo courtesy of the Steve Hardin Collection.*

CHAPTER XIII

McNelly Goes Into Action

THIRTEEN men lay on the grass of Brownsville Plaza
. . . all good dead men, each drilled through in various
vital spots with one or more bullets from a Winchester
or six-shooter.

They lay in a neat, military-like row, their wide open
eyes staring into the blue of the sky above, their heads
thrown back in grotesque attitudes . . . thirteen Mexican
banditti who nevermore would rise across the line to
lift the Texas cows.

An unlucky number it was—but it had been a luck-
less day for this small section of General Juan Cortina's
great cattle-thieving army. Even the chieftain of this
particular thieving band, Guadalupe Espinosa, himself,
lay among the dead; at the head of the column, where
a leader should be. That is, people pointed to the corpse
and called it that of the handsome robber. He was, in all
truth, a little hard to identify, even by such of his
friends who had crossed over from Matamoras to view
the gruesome display . . . the splat of a rifle bullet had
caught Señor Espinosa squarely in the face!

The Plaza was filled with spectators—among them
the citizens of the town, cowboys from outlying ranchos,
a few blue-coated cavalrymen from Uncle Sam's garrison
at Fort Brown, and at least half the male population
of Matamoras.

The Mexicans came in groups of tens and twenties,

glanced briefly and silently at their dead countrymen, and then turned sullen, furtive eyes on the seventeen big-hatted and high-booted men who stood guard over the bodies. These seventeen attracted, on the whole, about as much attention as the lately lamented on the green. They were all young, many of them scarcely more than beardless boys, but they looked hard—hard as nails—and the two forty-five-calibre Colt revolvers suspended from cartridge belts around each man's waist, did little to soften appearances. They leaned on their Winchesters in the careless fashion of men accustomed to reckless and bloody work—and they were just that, the thirteen on the grass being ample proof.

The leader of the band, a tall, black-haired young man who wore a mustache and an imperial, looked over the string of bodies and then turned to the spectators, his steely blue eyes searching among the Mexicans.

"If any relatives are here and want to claim a body," he said, in a quiet, even voice, "they may do so. My Rangers," he added, "are through with them."

The speaker waited, but no relative came forward. The dead apparently were deserted, even by their own kin. A sight-seer in the edge of the crowd nudged his neighbor, a soldier from the fort.

"Who is he?"

"Who is he?" The trooper looked at his questioner in amazement. "You ask me who HE is! Why, that's McNelly . . . Captain McNelly of the Texas Rangers . . . he's been out after cattle thieves!"

And then he told the story which, like an epic tale of fire and blood, already had swept over Brownsville and Matamoras. On the morning of the day before, June 12, 1875, Captain L. H. McNelly and his company of Rangers (there had been eighteen of them then) had picked up the trail of Guadalupe Espinosa's raiders in Cameron County as the Mexicans were driving for the border with two hundred and fifty head of stolen Texas cattle. They had caught up to the bandits, a party of fourteen, near the Laguna Madre, a swamp bit of ground near the line, and although the Mexicans had managed to get the cattle to a little hilltop on the opposite side of the marsh, Captain McNelly had ordered an immediate charge and the Rangers, with six-shooters in hand, had cut through the swamp under a volley of rifle fire from the elevated position held by the raiders.

One Ranger, L. S. Smith, had toppled from his horse during the opening fusillage and his companions, seeing him fall, had dug in their spurs and sped on, hell-bent for a swift and furious revenge—which they got, thirteen times over, in the hour's fight which followed. Espinosa's men, notoriously bad shots at their best (and worse when excited) tried a couple of more volleys, but seeing that they were ineffective, turned and fled, leaving the cattle herd on the hill.

They streaked for the Río Grande, but too late . . . the Rangers were down upon them before they could make a fair start; and in scarcely more time than it requires for the telling the scrap was over, with fourteen bodies strewn over the course of a mile's running fight. . . . Ranger Smith and the thirteen Mexicans. Not a single raider escaped; the fourteenth in the band, José

Marie Olguin, being so seriously wounded that he died later in the Cameron County jail. Some of Cortina's "best" were among the casuals—men like Pancho Lopez and Rafael Sabinas.

Espinosa was shot in the face by Captain McNelly himself. Early in the mad chase the bandit leader's horse had been winged by a bullet and Espinosa, thrown uninjured from the saddle, had sought refuge in the swamp. There McNelly had trailed him, engaged him in a rifle duel, and put a Winchester ball through his head.

The Rangers first took Smith to Brownsville for burial and then returned with a wagon for their victims —to spread them on the square as a morbid, pointed warning to the cattle bandits of Cortina's infamous brigade . . . thirteen dead men all in a row.

But there was something deeper in that grim gesture than merely a warning to bandits. The ranchers and the citizens of the town could see that . . . for there were troops at Fort Brown, and they had done little, or nothing, to help combat Don Juan's autocratic powers, although they realized as well as the stockmen that the mayor of Matamoras was surely and certainly draining the American side of its livestock resources.

So McNelly must have smiled to himself as he laid out the bodies on the Plaza. Time after time he had asked the troops for help, but had been turned down. Well, here was some of his own work; a good Ranger job, and perhaps it would serve to teach the cavalrymen a thing or two. That, he reasoned, was the proper way to deal with the situation on the border—with gunfire and sudden death.

And the thirty-year-old Ranger captain wasn't the only one who smiled. So did Sheriff James G. Browne of Cameron County, for only a dozen days before, in the absence of the Rangers, he had addressed the following letter to the fort:

"Brownsville, June 1, 1875.
General J. H. Potter, U. S. A.,
Commanding Fort Brown, Texas.

General—I received positive news this morning that a party of men from Mexico were going in the direction of the mouth of the Arroya Colorado in search of cattle. They seldom remain more than two or three days. Others, with myself, have made three unsuccessful trips, because I had not enough men to station in the rear while we went ahead. Captain McNelly, of the State Volunteer Troops, left for Corpus Christi last Thursday; therefore, I am obliged to call on you for assistance—say ten or twelve men, for two or three days. I am, General, very respectfully, your most obedient servant,
JAMES G. BROWNE,
Sheriff, Cameron County."

The letter had been returned with the following note from the officer in charge of the post:

"Headquarters, Fort Brown, June 2, 1875.
"Respectfully returned to the Sheriff of Cameron County, Texas, with the remark that, under recent instruction, I am not authorized to furnish troops as asked within.
MAJ. H. C. MERRIAM,
24th Cavalry, Temporarily Commanding Post."

Quite naturally, the sheriff was pleased. If the troops wouldn't help protect the ranching interests from the thieves, McNelly would—and could.

Don Juan, too, had begun to take notice of the young

Ranger captain. The boy was becoming a real thorn in the flesh, and through sources known only to himself he made inquiries. He learned this—

That McNelly, though young, was a hard man, who had been brought up in a hard school, and had crowded into three decades of life more blood-stirring adventure than usually falls to the lot of men three times his age. He was an aristocrat, reared in the tradition of the Southern gentleman, and he had fought his first battles at the age of seventeen—enlisting from Washington County as a private in the Texas Mounted Volunteers at the opening of the Civil War and serving in Sibley's Brigade of the Confederacy throughout the conflict.

He had been, always, a rabid rebel, and his daring at the front soon won for him a captain's commission over a scouting company in Colonel Tom Green's Texas regiment. Thin, pale, and perhaps already attacked by the ravishing malady which was to kill him, McNelly distinguished himself gloriously in the ranks of the South. He had turned spy to prowl about the Union lines; he had led his men in one strategical attack that brought home eight hundred Federal prisoners; his command, through bold and dashing work, had earned the title of "guerrillas"—and so it was little wonder that when McNelly came home in '65 he came to be looked upon as one of the greatest young soldiers that Texas had sent to the war. Men said that in the face of the enemy this youth from Washington County seemed to care not one iota whether he lived or died. He rode hard, and he fought like the devil, and he didn't get excited in the flame of battle. Young McNelly was, then, just the man that E. J. Davis, Republican Governor of Texas in Reconstruction days, wanted when, in 1870, he started about the business of selecting a commander for the Ranger forces to be put on the border in opposition to Cortina's ambitious cattle thieves. Governor Davis broached the subject, but McNelly merely laughed and refused.

"I won't work for a damned carpet-bagger," he had said, recalling that Davis had fought against him in Louisiana during the war. But McNelly's friends, some of them most bitter opponents of the governor, begged him to take the job.

"It won't be working for Davis," they said. "It will be working for the State, and you can do a real service."

And so, finally, McNelly was cajoled into taking the captaincy, picking a company of thirty-five men, some of whom had served with him during the war. He selected them carefully—Lieutenant L. B. Wright, Lieutenant T. J. Robinson, Sergeants J. B. Armstrong, R. P. Orrell, and George Hall. There were others—all young men, all hard, and with the scrapping spirit which only young men possess. They went south—to help Juan Cortina raise "hell on the border." But they went about it in a different manner from the Matamoras mayor.

McNelly knew that his men were strangers on the Río Grande and that they would not, until they had proved themselves, be respected. He tried to put himself for the moment, in Don Juan's shoes . . . tried to think as Cortina might be thinking. Would the general really pay much attention to the presence of thirty young Texas Rangers? With two or three thousand cut-throat thieves at his beck and call, Don Juan probably would laugh and pass it off as a huge joke. But McNelly would show him that the Rangers were tough hombres.

Accordingly, he gave orders to his men, immediately after arrival on the border, to make a thoroughgoing business of breaking up every Mexican fandango they could find either in Brownsville or Matamoras. And a thoroughgoing job they made of it. The Rangers would enter a building where a dance was in progress, shoot out the lights and then raise a general rumpus. Thus, in the two cities the popularity of the fandango diminished—but the Rangers won reputations as exceptionally hard-boiled eggs.

The captain's reasoning had been correct. The worst thief and the most desperate criminal has some respect for the majesty of the law, and the very fact that there existed an organized band of brave, armed men, soon struck a terror to the hearts of evildoers. A reputation established, McNelly went after the cattle thieves. He knew that his force was woefully small, and that without the aid of the military it could not guard every portion of the country at once, but with secret and rapid moves the captain wasn't long in making the word Ranger something to fear on the Río Grande.

But he was handicapped—for the reasons set out above—and Don Juan knew that as well as anyone, and so the general set his own spies to work and organized more closely the ramifications of his giant cattle-stealing machine. Notwithstanding obstacles, the small force did the best it could. For five years the Rangers rode the line; for five years they chased thieves and killed many men; for five years they tried, as best they could, to bring order out of chaos—and for five years the American army posts watched the show.

How many times had McNelly's Rangers, hot in pursuit of cattle rustlers, picked off a few with their rifles only to see the rest of the band drive a stolen herd across the river—where pursuit, under the rigid ban of international law, must stop. McNelly himself didn't know. He had ridden long, hard nights, slept in the rain and mud, lived on short rations, only to see the quarry scamper across the river to the safety of the Southern Republic. It had been, from 1870 to 1875, heart-breaking work.

Once he had written this despairing letter to the adjutant:

"With my present force I can do but little. These raids are made from seventy to one hundred miles from my camp, and by the time I receive information and get to the crossing, the raiders are over the Rio Grande and safe from my men, as at almost any point on the whole line of the river, from Matamoras to Piedras Negras, they can gather from one hundred to two hundred men to resist us if we attempt a crossing . . . it is too humiliating to follow the thieves to the bank of the river to see our stock on the opposite bank, and have the raiders defy us to cross—but crossing with my present force is almost certain destruction."

Was it any wonder, then, that the captain sweated under the collar? Was it any wonder that he used massacre methods when he *did* get a fair chance at any of Cortina's army—as in the case of Guadalupe Espinosa's men?

After what had occurred, after being checked at every

turning, was it any wonder that he looked with disdain on the dress-parading troopers of the garrisons? Five years on the line had raised the officer's temperature to the boiling point—and so he welcomed with particular pleasure Adjutant General Steele's report to the governor suggesting "orders to pursue and capture felons into Mexico, if necessary." That gave McNelly the break he wanted—he had sweated long enough . . .

CHAPTER XIV

The Rangers Invade Mexico!

ON THE 20th of November, 1875, the McNelly company—about thirty men in all—halted on the north bank of the Río Grande after chasing a band of Cortina's raiders to the water's edge. With them were two troops of the 8th U. S. Cavalry under Captain James Randlett and Captain H. J. Farnsworth—while on the south bank, just crawling from the river to thumb their noses at their pursuers, was a varied assortment of Mexican banditti, joyous over the success they had had in crossing two hundred and fifty head of cattle from the Santa Gertrudes ranch of Captain Richard King, foremost cattle baron of the border.

Captain McNelly didn't say much; he merely looked across to the Southern Republic with a wistful expression in his blue eyes. Juan Cortina, he told himself, wasn't going to get away with it this time. The captain, through his spies, knew exactly what Cortina was planning and where those beeves were going—first to the Rancho de los Cuevos, a bandit stronghold a few miles south of the line, and thence to Monterrey, with which city General Cortina had entered into a contract for the delivery of twenty thousand head of cattle within the next ninety days. The Santa Gertrudes cattle probably were the first of the collections to be made on the American side. He told his men and the army officers what he had learned, and then:

"I suppose we'd better go over and get them," suggested McNelly.

But Captain Randlett of the Eighth protested. Yes, he knew that Colonel Potter, commanding the Río Grande district, had promised the Rangers help but, even so, he couldn't move his command across the river until he had orders from his major.

"Then we'll go alone!" exclaimed McNelly, heatedly. "The colonel promised help, but I see I'm not going to get it." Then he turned to his own men and added: "Here's a real chance to even scores, and I'm going down to Rancho Cuevos to do it. It'll be hard fighting, because they'll be expecting us . . . but we can whip them. I know that. However, if any of you men want to stay behind, that's your business. You didn't enlist to fight in Mexico, you know. Anybody want to stay?"

Nobody did, and under the cover of darkness, the command moved across the Río Grande.

The captain and two men went first, in a boat, to scout the opposite bank, and then the rest made the crossing—five men taking over their horses.

Jesus Sandoval, the guide, was one of these, and had there been light enough to see, the Rangers would have observed in Sandoval's eyes a peculiar glint that boded no good for the enemy who crossed his trail that morning. For Jesus once had been a wealthy rancher on the American side, and Cortina's raiders had burned his home and ravished his wife and daughter . . . since then he had been with the Rangers, dealing out such death and destruction as he could.

The cavalrymen on the American side watched as the

night engulfed the little band. Some of the younger officers wished that they might go along, but they knew only too well the strict orders from Secretary of War Belknap—no invasion, and strict neutrality of the border. The troopers listened; they could hear, across the narrow stretch of water, the Ranger officers talking to their men—and then silence. They knew that the advance on Rancho de los Cuevas had started.

McNelly had acted with characteristic speed once his force had reached the south bank. He had sent the five horsemen out as an advance scouting party with orders to "shoot at everything that moved." The detachment started, Jesus Sandoval cocking back the hammer of his Winchester. He used it, and to good advantage, a short time later; for at the gates of the rancho the five Rangers were challenged by seven Mexican sentries.

—Their bodies were still in the gateway as the twenty-five men on foot entered, to make the attack on Cuevos.

But even as Captain McNelly had predicted, the gentlemen who occupied the bandit stronghold, were ready and waiting, the first greeting for the American visitors coming in the form of a fusillade fired from the corrals, and followed by a fast-charging "welcoming committee" made up of vaqueros and rurales of Cortina's brigade.

The Rangers barely had time to scatter for cover as the first wave came galloping to the attack.

"Pick your man!" sang out Captain McNelly. "I'll kill the leader!"

He raised his rifle and squeezed the trigger. A rurale toppled from the saddle. Other Winchesters cracked from the brush on the captain's right and left . . . and the rurales turned and retreated for the safety of the rancho—but with several empty saddles.

A wounded horse made the early morning hideous with its cries, and from several positions in the corrals came the sobbing moan of wounded men. The Rangers weren't wasting any lead, and it was indeed a sad business for the bandit who lifted his head above the stockade.

But Captain McNelly was worried. Here he was with thirty men on an invasion of Mexico, and only five of them mounted. He might be in a trap—and suspected that he was—if the enemy only knew it. He called Sergeant George Hall (the same Hall who had spied for him on Cortina's cattle boat at Bagdad) and instructed him to reconnoitre and ascertain, if possible, the strength of the opposition.

Crawling on his belly, Hall crept forward, protected by the Winchesters of the Rangers, who kept up a popping fire at every Mexican who dared show so much as a hat brim. Within ten minutes Hall was back.

"About ten to one," he told McNelly.

"Then we'd better get out," said the captain. "Pass the word to the men to retire to the river and make a stand. Those with horses will protect the rear as we move back."

The company retired slowly and the Mexicans, fearing a trap, were cautious about following; so the Rangers

were able to intrench on the banks of the Río Grande—
still on the Mexican side—with only one horse wounded.
It was then that the trailing enemy grew bolder and
swept down for an assault, but it was the Rangers who
had the advantage this time, and every flash of a Winchester across the sands dropped a man . . . dead or
wounded . . . in the brush. Three times the bandits
stormed, but three times they were repulsed.

In the meantime McNelly had received reinforcements. The younger officers of the Eighth Cavalry,
watching from the opposite shore, could stand hitched
no longer. They whipped off their shoulder straps and
their eagle-embossed buttons and came whooping over
the water to join in the mêlée; and even those who
didn't come opened up with their rifles from the American side, firing over the heads of the Rangers.

It was at this juncture that Captain McNelly
received a message that made his blood fairly boil—that
made him more angry than all the bullets zipped in his
direction during the morning. One of the army officers
brought it over—a message received by the detachment
a few minutes before from Colonel Potter.

And McNelly's face grew red, and even redder, as
his eyes followed down the lines:

"To Major Alexander,
Commanding at the Front:

Advise Captain McNelly to return at once to this side of
the river. Inform him that you are directed not to support
him in any way while he remains on Mexican territory. If
McNelly is attacked by Mexican forces on Mexican ground,
do not render him any assistance. Keep your forces in the

*position you now hold and await further orders. Let me know
if McNelly acts upon your advice and returns.*

POTTER,
Commanding district of the Río Grande.
By order of the Secretary of War."

He fished in his pocket, found a piece of paper and
a pencil, and framed an immediate reply, which he read
to his men before he took it, personally, across the
border to file on the wire. This is what he wrote:

"To Colonel J. H. Potter,
U. S. A.,
Fort Brown, Texas.
*   I shall remain in Mexico with my Rangers until tomorrow
morning, perhaps longer, and shall cross the Río Grande at
my own discretion. Give my compliments to the Secretary of
War and tell him the United States troops may go to hell.*

L. H. McNELLY,
Commanding Texas State Troops, Mexico."

The captain didn't spend much time across the border
—just enough to dispatch "his compliments"—and then
he returned to the Mexican side to find that the Mexicans, weary of the sniping engagement, were ready to
make terms . . . any kind of terms to get the Rangers
out of Mexico.

The spokesman had come forward under a flag of
truce, protested that the Texans already had killed
twenty-seven of their number and had wounded many
more. Would Captain McNelly state the terms for with-
drawal? The captain would—the condition being prompt
return to the Texas side of the cattle lately crossed.

The Mexicans said it sounded like a fair bargain, and
forthwith signed an agreement promising to deliver the

herd early next morning across from Río Grande City, where the animals then were penned. Under this pact McNelly retired to the American side and waited for morning.

But in the morning it was a different story. The Mexicans, having received word that a regiment of cavalry was advancing from Monterrey, expressed regret to the Rangers and excused themselves from delivery on grounds that it was not proper to transact business on Sunday, that day being the Sabbath.

But McNelly had his blood up. He had invaded Mexico once—he would do it again; and so, with his Rangers behind him, he rode across to the stock pens, which were strongly guarded by Mexican cavalrymen, and renewed his demands. But here another impasse. Mexican customs officials appeared and said that duty must be paid on the animals before they could cross. That, with the captain, was the last straw.

"Duty, hell!" he roared, as some of his men cocked their Winchesters. "You ask duty on cattle stolen in Texas! I'll give you damned scoundrels just ten minutes to get those cattle started toward the border!"

The cattle crossed—duty free—and the cavalrymen, not the Rangers, did the driving. A great deal may be accomplished in ten minutes . . . sometimes.

That was the beginning of the end of Don Juan's tryannical reign of thievery on the border. The Rangers, and a mere handful of them, had succeeded where the army had failed; and the gentle mayor-general of Matamoras no longer smiled his suave, white-toothed smile . . . for he knew that McNelly, having once set a precedent, would not hesitate to follow it up; and McNelly didn't. At "his own discretion" he crossed and recrossed the line time and time again, and he usually brought back cattle that carried the iron burns of Texas owners.

Cuba received little more meat from Bagdad, and Monterrey hungered for beefsteak with a Texas flavor.

The Rangers had proved to Don Juan that he wasn't the only one who could raise the proverbial "hell on the border."

Read these paragraphs, still on file among the laconic reports of the Adjutant General's office. They have to do with McNelly's company:

"December, 1875—On 28th, a scouting party came across a slaughter house for stolen beeves about forty miles north of Las Kuscias. Ranchero in charge arrested. After an ineffectual attempt to bribe the sergeant, he tried to escape, and was killed in the attempt.

"January, 1876—On 30th, detachment tried unsuccessfully to find trail of Mexicans who stole seventeen head of horses near San Nicolas Ranch.

"May, 1876—On 17th, five miles from Edinburg, company struck a party of four Mexicans crossing stolen cattle. Killed two, badly wounded one, recovered seven head of cattle and captured six horses, with equipments. *This was done while the Mexican General, Escobedo, was dining with U. S. officers at Edinburg, and within sound of Escobedo's brass band of twenty pieces.* Captain McNelly called upon Captain H. J. Farnsworth, Eighth U. S. Cavalry, who refused to cross the border and secure the stolen cattle. Captain McNelly then crossed into Mexico with three men, searched within one and one-half miles of Escobedo's lines, but did not find any cattle. Captain McNelly then went to the Alcalde of Reynosa and demanded return of the cattle and thieves. He promised both, but nothing was done. *The impression prevails that the cattle were for Escobedo's troops.*

"June, 1876—On 4th, arrested King Fisher and nine of his gang. On 6th, King Fisher and gang released while Captain McNelly was on his way with witnesses. Seven of the nine could have been indicted for murder in several cases. Had between six hundred and eight hundred head of stolen cattle and horses, which were turned loose."

That last item reveals just one more part of the day's work for the Rangers; it proves, too, that legal technicalities often favored the criminal and hampered the work of the officer . . . for that brief report to the Adjutant contains a longer story than its lines might indicate.

King Fisher was an A-1 bad man, one of the very worst that the border produced—worse, if possible, than the slashers under Cortina. At his ranch he had gathered together the most villainous and bloodthirsty gang of cutthroats he could muster, and they took what they wanted . . . running a stiff competition to the Mexicans in the gentle art of cattle lifting. But one day McNelly rode up to King's ranch with a squad of Rangers behind him and informed King that, if he resisted arrest, he would be shot down like any other rattlesnake.

The company took a choice lot of King's crew into Edinburg and then set out to find witnesses. Returning two days later, they met Fisher and his merry fellows in the road and rearrested them. But King showed the papers for his bail and there was nothing to do but let him go. The captain's only comment was that if the people of the Río Grande district wanted to let a red-handed murderer run loose in their midst it was their own funeral. He warned the cattle thief, however, not to cross his path again.

They didn't meet again—for that same year McNelly, broken in health from long exposure, retired from the Rangers. Within another twelve months he was dead at the age of thirty-three—one of the youngest, but yet one of the greatest of the bold captains who rode the wild border.

He was buried in Washington County and the tall granite shaft under which he lies was erected by one of his most devoted admirers, Captain Richard King, whose broad cattle empire on the Río Grande McNelly helped to guard . . . and to save for a posterity which includes Richard Kleberg, the present Congressman.

The Ranger company carried on—but McNelly's spirit led it.

Captain John Armstrong. *Photo courtesy of the Texas Ranger Hall of Fame and Museum, Waco, Texas.*

CHAPTER XV

The Rangers Capture John Wesley Hardin

In OTHER states in olden days when outlaws jumped their bonds, or hurried on to parts unknown to dodge the long reach of the law, presiding judges of the courts sat down and wrote but two small letters on the public ledgers—"G. T."

Which meant, in clearer language, "Gone to Texas."

Two small letters, but singularly suggestive—for there was a time when Texas had that kind of reputation. It was, for many, many years a sanctuary for all bad actors who drifted south when other precincts grew too warm; and with the advent of this sinister migration it was only natural that Texas felt called upon, as a matter of state pride, to find among her sons a few fast-triggered gents capable of carrying on the local honors.

Such a champion was acquired on May 26, 1853, when the stork called at the parsonage of the Reverend Mr. Hardin and left a son, who almost immediately was christened after the greatest of all the Methodists, John Wesley, the founder of the church. Before the passing of many years, however, it became apparent that the well-meaning bird had made a most grievous error in leaving this particular child in the home of a minister of the gospel . . . for John Wesley Hardin, before reaching the tender age of fifteen years, had killed a man —a negro trooper whose actions in about the town of Bonham had not been to the young man's fancy.

135

The good minister, of course, was aghast; but it was not until his son had engaged in several similar high-spirited escapades that he became more or less convinced that a tiger had gotten in among the family sheep. He prayed long prayers, but all in vain—for a tiger, once given a taste of blood, usually comes back for more, and that old fact became startlingly evident in the case of Mr. Wesley's doughty namesake.

The fear of monotony precludes any attempt to trace the hectic early history of young John Wesley—so suffice it to say that somewhere he picked up an unusually good brace of single-action, 41-calibre Colt revolvers, which he used to such glorious personal advantage that when he came to live in the town of Cuero in the early '70s he already had earned the right to ridge the gun handles with ten or fifteen notches.

He didn't, of course, do any such thing, for the professional in his line of business invariably preferred not to advertise too blatantly; but Mr. Hardin wasn't long in Cuero before his fame became choice local gossip of the whispered variety, and the young men of the town took pains not to get in his way when he decided to walk abroad.

The small boys of the place looked upon him as a sort of super bogey-man, but all the same they didn't miss an opportunity to watch the dapper Texan twirl his pistols in the famous "border roll." He was a fancy gun handler, the most adroit of all his contemporaries, and to see Hardin whirl those two heavy Colts on his nimble fingers, jerking back the hammers as they turned, was, indeed, something to write home about.

Once he had used his subtle artistry to disarm Wild Bill Hickok, the prince of pistoleers, when that great man was city marshal of Abilene, the Kansas cattle terminal—and that event alone was enough to reserve for him a high place in the gunman's hall of fame.

When he went to Abilene behind a herd of Texas longhorns, Hardin knew full well that the town had an ordinance against gun-totin' and that Wild Bill was zealous in its enforcement, but that didn't prevent him from going into the municipality with the two .41s swinging at his hips.

Marshal Hickok spotted him almost immediately.

"You'll have to hand over those shooting-irons," he said. "We've got a law against 'em up here."

And Hardin offered them, butts first, but as the marshal reached to take them John Wesley executed an expert "border roll," clicked back the hammers and left the surprised Wild Bill staring into two dark muzzles.

"Unbuckle your belt and drop your holsters!" ordered the Texan—and Wild Bill did.

That's the kind of tough *hombre* Wes Hardin had turned out to be. His name enters this narrative only for the purpose of showing the type of bad men, aside from the Comanche and the Mexican, that the Texas Rangers were called upon to combat in those wild, disordered days when the Frontier Battalion was attempting to make the state a decent place in which to live. And when his story is finished none other need be told— for he was the worst of the lot.

Briefly, here are a few of the naughty pranks that are

scored on the ledger against this mischievous son of a
Methodist minister:

Emerging with a crony one day from a Cuero saloon,
he espied a stranger sitting in a chair against a building
front two blocks down the street. Mr. Hardin, suddenly possessed of a bright idea, turned to his companion.

"You say you think I'm drunk?" he sneered. "Tell
you what I'll do," he said, pointing at the stranger down
the street. "I'll bet I can knock 'im over with a single
shot."

His crony called the wager, and Hardin drew the
right-hand .41 Colt. He fired but once . . . and then
reentered the saloon to collect his bet, a whisky straight.

Another time, as he went to bed in a small rooming
house, the rumbling snores of another guest in an adjoining room disturbed his rest. The outraged Mr. Hardin
guessed at the position of the snorer on the opposite side
of the thin partition, placed one of his revolvers within
six inches of the wall, and fired. The guess was good, and
Wes turned over and went to sleep . . . dead men
don't snore.

Incidents like that, and many more . . . enough, in
fact, to fill a sizeable Saga of the Six-shooter, especially
after he had decided to capitalize on his reputation as the
"greatest gunman in Texas," and take up the wholesale
end of the trade. And concerning this, witness an excerpt
from the report Adjutant General Britton sent to Governor E. J. Davis for the year 1873:

"In Gonzales County there is a strong band of thieves
and murderers headed by John Hardin, alias Wesley,
who is reported to have committed sixteen different

murders, and had threatened to kill a member of the Legislature, the Hon. S. T. Robb. One thousand dollars reward has been offered by Your Excellency for Hardin, and one thousand by the State of Missouri.

"On the 22nd day of March this man Hardin with a squad of twelve men, all armed with Winchester guns and six-shooters, rode into the town of Gonzales and delivered the county jail of all its prisoners, threatening the guard with death if they made any alarm. The sheriff of Gonzales County informs me that he has made no effort to arrest any of these parties; that the citizens will not answer his summons (for posses); and that the outlaws would be released, even if caught and placed in jail.

"I think I am justified in stating," added the Adjutant, "that not less than one hundred men are prowling about the state in gangs of twelve to twenty, murdering and robbing almost without restraint."

Wes Hardin had called the bluff of the citizenry and had gotten away with it. They were afraid of him— but the Rangers weren't. Already, standing orders were out to bring him in—"dead or alive."

And he was alive when the Rangers brought him in— this man who disarmed Wild Bill, first prince of pistoleers. Three men from the McNelly company did it— Sergeant John Armstrong, Charles McKinney and John Duncan.

The Ranger force at that time had its hands full. The Comanches were raiding in the west, the Mexicans were stealing cattle on the border, and John Wesley had something of an open hand in his forays about the country. The years 1875 and 1876 brought this son of a minister to the height of his murderous career, but after each crime he dashed for a hiding place in the western hills, secure in the knowledge that McNelly was too busy on the Border, and the other captains too busy on the Indian frontier to take up the long trail they must follow to run him down. But even if an expedition couldn't be sent to track him, the order for arrest on sight was out just the same.

And so when McNelly had put the quietus on Cortina's bandits and had retired to die, the men of his company, granted at last a breathing spell, came to look upon Mr. Hardin's career as a piece of unfinished business. It made no difference that Wes evidently had departed from the state; he was a marked man, and wanted. The Rangers set a trap to catch him, and it worked.

Preacher Hardin was living at that time on a West Texas ranch and so Ranger Duncan hid his star, hired out to an adjoining ranchman, and took it upon himself to make friends with the minister. He succeeded, and by the mathematical process of putting two and two together, learned that Wes was in Pensacola, Florida, where he had taken a bride to help share his ill-gotten Texas wealth. Ranger Duncan lost no time. He looked up Armstrong and McKinney and the three set out for the peninsular state.

After searching about Pensacola they located Mr. and Mrs. Hardin boarding a train at the railroad station. They entered a coach that was practically empty and took a seat. The Rangers let them settle down and then

Sergeant Armstrong entered the front of the coach after his two fellow officers had taken the chair directly behind the Hardins.

Armstrong walked slowly down the aisle and as he drew up alongside the unsuspecting pair he stopped, looked at the outlaw like a man recognizing an old friend, smiled and exclaimed:

"Well, if it isn't John Wesley Hardin! How are you, Wes?"

The bad man went for one of his guns, but the two Rangers behind him had anticipated the move. One of them nailed down his arms while the other took his six-shooters. Sergeant Armstrong snapped on the handcuffs —and that was all.

The Rangers didn't even wait for extradition papers. They stayed on that same train, which was headed out in a westerly direction, and they brought their prisoner straight to Texas. Of course, the story got out, and all along the way people met the train in hopes of catching a glimpse of the notorious bad actor.

They tried Wes in the courts, convicted him of murder, and sentenced him to twenty-five years in the state penitentiary at Huntsville where he utilized his spare time with the study of law so that he had a new profession at his fingertips when Governor Hogg pardoned him at the end of seventeen years. John Wesley went to Cuero and opened practice, but he didn't stay there long. He drifted west to El Paso, a brace of new revolvers supplanting the old .41s.

There still are men in that city of the West who knew Wes Hardin, and they say that prison softened him.

Perhaps so, but he wasn't entirely mellowed . . . for on the afternoon of August 19, 1895, he came face to face with one John Selman whose son, a member of the police force, had recently arrested Hardin's girl during that gentleman's absence from the city.

"Selman," said the bad man, "you've got a son who's a cowardly ——— ——— — ———!"

"Which one?" asked the old man, for he had more than one son.

"The one who works on the police force."

"No man can talk about any of my children like that and get away with it!" shouted Selman, adding a few choice estimations of Hardin's own character. "You're armed and I'm not . . . but I'm going home and get my gun, and I'm coming back shootin'."

"Go and get your gun," retorted Wes, "and when you come back I'll run you around the block like a wolf."

An hour later Hardin was standing at the bar of the Acme Saloon rolling dice with a companion for the drinks. The door opened and John Selman entered with a friend. Later, when they were called to testify, none of the spectators agreed on what had occurred, except that when the smoke cleared away Hardin lay at the end of the bar—a bullet hole through the back of his head, his revolver still in the holsters.

Selman, who previously had asked the police not to interfere because "this is a private matter between me and Hardin," was tried for murder and acquitted. He had a good lawyer—Albert B. Fall, who at that time never dreamed of becoming Secretary of the Interior.

Thus John Wesley Hardin went to join the twenty-five or thirty souls he had sent before him. He lay in state at Ross' Undertaking Parlors for several days before they carried him out to Concordia cemetery; and, as one of the El Paso newspapers of the day reported, "he looked natural and the features were in good shape."

A hard man and a cold-blooded killer, this Mr. Hardin, but the Texas Rangers softened him a bit—as they softened many another like him in the days which have come down through history as the outlaw era.

John Wesley Hardin. *Photo courtesy of the Steve Hardin Collection.*

Texas Rangers with Captain John R. Hughes seated at right. ca. 1900. *Photo courtesy of the Texas Ranger Hall of Fame and Museum, Waco, Texas.*

CHAPTER XVI

Captain John R. Hughes ... Border Boss

THERE is an old saying on the Mexican Border that "one Ranger is worth a hundred soldiers."

Its origin has been lost, but whoever first said it must have been thinking of Captain John R. Hughes, "border boss" in the '80s and one of the boldest Texas Rangers ever to toss an empty cartridge into the waters of the Río Grande.

He is one of the few old-timers of the service still alive, and these days he commutes between his bank at Austin and a ranch near El Paso in a 1924 model Ford— an erect, white-bearded old gentleman who walks with the springy step of a colt, and who possesses two of the blackest eyes you are likely to find in the length and breadth of Texas.

He is what they call in that part of the country a "well-to-do man," and he probably could buy a dozen limousines if he wanted them, but he still prefers the old Ford for his thirty-day drives from Austin to El Paso— thirty days because he has so many friends to visit on the way.

One thing more—he can outpace with little trouble the average young man of today; and it is noticeable that he carries his right arm with the elbow slightly crooked, the index finger of the hand extended—and if you're not familiar with the meaning of that gesture, ask some old-time Texan.

For the purpose of illustration let us drop back a few years . . . to the late '80s . . . and witness a street scene in a little town down on the Río Grande. On one side of the street stood a Mexican, one of the gay caballeros of the border, dressed in a high straw sombrero, a leather jacket, and a pair of fancy breeches, the legs of which were tucked into brown boot tops. He tapped occasionally the butt of a pearl-handled revolver that pepped from under the jacket, twirled his black mustache and announced to all and sundry that he wasn't afraid of any Ranger who ever rode a horse.

He had come to town, he said, looking for trouble, and he might go out and hunt it. He might, he added after about the third drink of mescal, go out and put a bullet hole in Ranger Captain Hughes. This was Victor Ochoa, known as the hardest Mexican on the border—wanted, even then, by the Mexican government for heading an uprising and for smuggling arms.

The borderland buzzed with excitement, for everybody knew that Mexico had asked Texas to capture Ochoa, and that Captain Hughes had been assigned to the job. And wasn't it a strange coincidence (or was it that) which brought Hughes into Fort Stockton just as this *hombre muy valiente* was making his loudest boasts?

Anyhow, there he stood, just across the street from Ochoa—a sort of smile on his face, his right elbow slightly crooked, and the index finger of his hand extended. Near-by loafers moved for cover, with the ambling gait of leisurely men in a hurry; the captain himself started across the narrow thoroughfare.

Ochoa stood his ground. He threw back his shoulders, dropped his hand to his gun-butt and waited. Hughes strode toward him, his coal-black eyes boring into the Mexican, his elbow still crooked. Breathlessly, the spectators waited for the draw, but it didn't come. Hughes walked on. A pace apart and Ochoa's nerve broke; his eyes fell.

"I want you, Victor," said the Ranger captain, quietly, as he plucked the Mexican's six-shooter from the holster.

"*Esta bueno, señor,*" Ochoa replied, surrendering meekly.

It was incidents like that, perhaps, which led the people on the Río Grande to observe that "one Ranger is worth a hundred troops."

In a way, Captain Hughes entered the Rangers with a pistol blazing in his hand. He came to Texas from Kansas in the '70s and settled near Liberty Hill, north of Austin, to earn his living breaking wild horses for sale, and it wasn't long until he had quite a remuda of outlaw mustangs in the corrals on the lot behind the ranch house, but one day some bold, bad men from the west paid the place a nocturnal call and took advantage of the "tenderfoot" from the plains of Kansas . . . for when Mr. Hughes awoke in the morning he discovered all his horses were missing, including Moscow, his favorite.

Hughes visited his neighbors and found that they, too, had lost their best horses to the band of raiders, and so he made a neighborly deal—he would go after the livestock and bring them back, if they would give him half of those he recaptured. The neighbors were only too glad to agree and Hughes, after lassoing a wild colt, took up the trail.

It was a long, hard ride that he started that day, more than a thousand miles and a year long, but he stuck on the trail clear across the plains of West Texas and into the ranch lands of New Mexico. There, he found his stolen horses and the men who took them; and, after a year's absence, he returned to the precincts of Liberty Hill with some of the horses and the sale price of those he had sold in New Mexico. He told his neighbors that the thieves had been well cared for; that four were dead, and the other two in the New Mexico penitentiary.

That event precipitated John Hughes into the Texas Rangers and in 1887 he enlisted at Georgetown to start a career that would make him the half-veiled hero of Zane Grey's Lone Star Ranger. He served for twenty-eight years, and most of that on the Mexican border.

The young private soon made enemies, notably the bandit brothers Carrasco—Matilde, Antonio and Florencio. While working at the Shafter mine, near Presidio del Norte, guarding the diggings against ore thieves from across the border, Hughes' detachment fought an engagement with the bandits, killing Matilde Carrasco, and for his part in the affair Hughes was made a sergeant, and given a post at Alpine.

From that day on he led a busy and eventful, not to mention dangerous, life. The Carrascos had loved their late brother and they swore an oath to settle matters with the sergeant. They raided—merely for the purpose, one suspects, of laying a trap for the Ranger, and though they tried with all the enthusiasm of revengeful Latins, they always failed to get their man; and as the weeks and the months rolled by the tables became reversed, with Hughes the hunter and the Carrascos the hunted.

And then Florencio got drunk—fatally drunk . . . at least it turned out that way.

Sergeant Hughes and Private Oden trailed a horse thief into Presidio and had just arrested him when news was brought to them that Florencio Carrasco was just galloping out of town. The Rangers caught up with him outside the town and a bullet from Oden's rifle knocked the Mexican from his horse. Hughes then finished the job, beating the bandit to the rifle draw and putting two bullets through him.

Thus died Florencio—and now there was one, Antonio. But the last of the Carrascos evidently thought better of continuing the feud. He was seen no more on the border; until he chose the wrong side in a revolution and was put "against the wall" at Ojinaga.

But in the wake of the Carrascos came the Olguins— Jesus Marie, the father; Sebastian, Severo and Priscellano, the brothers—four of the toughest over-the-border raiders who ever lifted a Texas steer. They settled on Pirate Island, a plot of ground neither Mexican nor American in the middle of the Río Grande opposite the Texas town of Ysleta; and using this convenient no-man's-land as a base, they started bloody excursions into the Texas countryside.

Matters drifted from bad to worse, and as the population of Ysleta, being principally Mexican, was in sympathy with the outlaws, the Texas Rangers decided to take a hand in the affairs of Pirate Island.

Sergeant Hughes still was at Alpine, but the main body of his company, under command of Captain Frank Jones, was stationed in Ysleta, where almost daily they ignored the threats of the citzenry, who hurled insults from the windows and set dogs upon the Ranger horses as they passed down the streets.

Jones considered that he had tarried long enough; it was high time to clean the island and teach the "buccaneers" a needed lesson, and so he organized a raid— one of those quiet, swift night affairs which the Rangers conducted so successfully. They went over and found the few small houses of the place deserted, but they found what they had gone to find—a fight. It occurred on the way back, when two Mexican horsemen sprang suddenly from covert and galloped away, the Rangers in pursuit. But that was all a part of a well-arranged trick, the two riders leading the company to the Mexican side of the river where a strongly intrenched ambush party lay in wait. Too late Captain Jones saw the mistake and then he ordered a retreat. His men rode back through a crackling hail of bullets to the American side, but Captain Jones did not ride with them. He lay on the Mexican side, near one of the three small huts of the village of Tres Jacales, where the ambush had been set.

Then the Olguins rallied their Pirate Island forces and challenged the Rangers to cross and get the body which, finally, was surrendered after forty-eight hours of argument. Ranger Bob Ross of El Paso was the man who went over to bring it back. The border seethed with hatred—on both sides of the river.

It was not long until the news of the affair came to Sergeant Hughes of Alpine, and immediately he set out for Ysleta. He took command, engaged the services of an ex-Ranger to act as spy for the company, and set about collecting what information he could as to the identity of the bandits who had trapped Captain Jones. And the spy, who had lived long enough along the border to impersonate a Mexican like a native, was not long in securing a lengthy list of names. St. Leon, for that was his name, fixed the principal blame on the brothers Olguin—and then things began to hum around Ysleta and Pirate Island. Hughes, who had received his captain's commission, was out for blood.

Organizing his men for a swift and driving raid, he went over to get the Olguins. Two men to a house they rushed down on the criminal settlement, battered in doors and then, with guns in hand, jumped into the 'dobe houses to surprise their "birds" in bed. It takes something more than an excess of cold, hard nerve to rush into a strange, dark room in the dead of night, especially when it is known that the room contains men wanted by the law, but that's what Hughes' Rangers did in their drive on Pirate Island; and on the very first raid they made a nice-sized catch, which included several men wanted for murder on the Texas side.

They didn't stop at one raid, either. They followed with one after another until the islet in the Río Grande was as clean as a hound's tooth. Nor did they take all captive—they killed seventeen of the twenty men the spy had written on the Jones murder list!

But the Olguins got away. Needless to say, however, they caused no more trouble on that section of the border.

Captain Hughes spent the remainder of his long service on the Río Grande and after the affair at the island only one guess was needed as to who was "boss of the border" in that particular section . . . for one glance from those black eyes of the captain usually was quite enough to tame the Mexican who carried a guilty conscience; and all along the river there are kicked-in doors which attest to his passing.

It was Captain Hughes and Ranger Thalis Cook who, in 1896, rounded up three train robbers who were laying in wait for the Southern Pacific near Alpine. They flushed the gang, headed by Bert Umphries, in the hills and in the fight which followed Cook killed two with a Winchester. Umphries escaped to be captured a short time afterward.

The Cortina raids were practically over when Captain Hughes went on duty, but small, scattered bands of marauders still ravaged the countryside, and since the Mexican-dominated border populace was so thoroughly in sympathy with the lawless element, it is nothing short of remarkable that entire companies, much less one Ranger, lived to tell the tale in later years.

Perhaps they couldn't have survived had they had a title other than "Ranger"—for even now there is a sort of magic about the word. There is something about it that marks the man so titled as an element apart from the general term officer; something that marks him in the public mind as a super-law enforcer. And there is something more than men behind it all; there is a tradition, and each man—like Captain John Hughes—contributes some part to that tradition.

The Rangers didn't bear charmed lives—they merely had a reputation.

Captain Hughes today leads an easy-going life; but his remarkable energy defies you to guess his age at seventy-seven. He spends part of his time with the family of his nephew, Emery H. Hughes, with whom he is associated in the Citizens Industrial Bank at Austin, and part—particularly the winter months—with old border friends near El Paso. He has no family of his own—he never married.

But he has more friends than most men have, despite the border enemies of long ago. That's why he takes thirty days by auto from Austin to El Paso. He is there every winter, idling in the sun and talking to old friends ... the tires removed from his 1924 Ford and the wheels jacked up pending the advent of spring.

He is quiet, even reticent, when it comes to relating the highlights of his interesting career. He prefers to let others do the talking, even about himself.

A wealthy and an aging man, he doesn't worry much about the present crop of gangsters and the modern kidnaper. He merely smiles.

"I've seen worse," he says. "Why worry?"

He doesn't. And besides, he still walks as he always walked—with the elbow slightly crooked and the index finger of the hand extended. . . .

Captain Bill McDonald. *Photo courtesy of the Texas Ranger Hall of Fame and Museum, Waco, Texas.*

CHAPTER XVII

Captain Bill McDonald ... Riot Buster

THERE was trouble in Dallas.

A prize fight had been scheduled, and since there was a state law making ring encounters illegal, the town was divided against itself over whether the affair should come off as planned. Fearing serious disturbances on fight night, some of those among the citizenry had asked the governor to send Texas Rangers.

And so, on the day of the event Captain Bill McDonald, lanky, white-mustached state trooper, who spoke with a slow drawl in his voice, dropped off the train in Dallas. He was met by the mayor. His Honor was glad to see the Captain, but he appeared worried as he looked up and down the platform.

"Where," he asked, "are your Rangers?"

"Hell!" exclaimed Captain McDonald, "you've only got one prize fight, haven't you?"

And there was no trouble in Dallas that night. That was the manner in which McDonald handled bad situations in the late 1890s and early 1900s—by himself, or with very few men at his back. And he got away with it . . . the longshoremen's strike at Port Arthur in 1902 being another case in point.

The dock workers had walked out and had made it plain that they would not allow strike-breakers to go on the job. McDonald arrived with four men of Company B and confronted the mob.

"How many men you got?" shouted the strike leader.

"Five, including myself," said Captain McDonald.

"Then it stands four hundred against five," estimated the striker, sizing up his opponent.

"Four hundred against five," drawled the Ranger captain. "Well, that makes it about even."

Peace reigned in Port Arthur.

Dallas and Port Arthur were not exceptions by any means. McDonald and his men made the same kind of history all over the state. He had behind him, he knew, the tradition and the reputation of the Texas Ranger, and he made the most of it—but he had something else, too. He was known as the best quick-on-the-draw, rapid-firing revolver shot in Texas. At fifty paces, it was said, he could shoot the spot from the ace of spades and send the second bullet through the hole; he could wing a flying bird with the six-shooter, or smash the eagle on a high-tossed dollar; and, compared with these small-sized targets, the body of a man made an almost unmissable mark.

It was not, then, a question of whether Captain McDonald would hit a man—but where. Thus the deadly accuracy of his Colt became known in Texas from the Río Grande to the Panhandle.

And he had a certain psychology in his handling of the pistol. For he used to say that:

"No man in the wrong can stand up against a fellow who's in the right and keeps on a-coming."

That's the motto that he used when, in the early part of 1891, he set out for the northwest to clean up the lawless element on the plains and in the Panhandle.

Captain William Jess McDonald was born in Mississippi in 1852, moving when a young man to Mineola, Wood County, Texas, where in due course of time fate decreed that he should wear a deputy sheriff's badge, and it was here that he became friends with James Hogg, who later was to be the governor and make Bill a Ranger captain. In 1883 the young Mississippian removed to Wichita Falls and went into the lumber business, which he sold two years later after filing claim on a tract of land in Hardeman County, near Quanah, then little more than a wild and woolly western settlement on the Red River frontier.

It wasn't long before he became a deputy United States marshal with the dangerous Panhandle area of "No Man's Land" his ranging ground—a great unfenced penitentiary which had become the rallying place for the more vicious fugitives of justice from both Texas and the Indian Territory. Here he fought and beat into submission many outlaws, but it was not until he had walked into the camp of Dan and Bob Campbell and captured them both, two of the worst bad men of the area, that his fame as a single-handed bandit-nemesis became widespread.

Shortly after McDonald had landed these two gentlemen in jail at Wichita Falls, he learned that S. A. McMurray had resigned as captain of Company B, Texas Rangers, and so Bill lost no time getting down to Austin to see his old friend, Governor Hogg.

He walked into the executive office, and, after the usual formalities of greeting, Hogg asked the officer what he could do for him.

"Well," said McDonald, "I heard that McMurray had quit. . . . I'm here to take his place."

Hogg didn't hesitate, and that January day in 1891 Bill McDonald walked out of the governor's office with a Ranger captain's commission in his pocket . . . headed for the Panhandle for one of the biggest jobs of man-taming an officer ever was called upon to perform.

If you hold any erroneous belief that that country, the former hunting ground of the Comanche, wasn't a rip-roaring place in those days, look up some man who lived there and let him tell you. The Indian was gone; the cowboy was king; and the cattle thief was "grand vizier." It was a land of cattle kingdoms, great ranches sprawling over miles and miles of prairie—and the six-shooter was the sceptre used to rule the domains.

The cowboy, sober, wasn't such a bad sort; but the cowboy, drunk, was a different kind of hombre . . . and when they came into the towns for periodical sprees after months of lonely riding on the plains, they usually found enough trouble to make things merry for a long while to come. The average cowboy wasn't a bad actor at heart; just reckless, but when he did bring out his six-gun he could shoot. The cattle thief and the outlaw of those times was, in most cases, the cowboy gone bad— he lifted herds and drove them to the Territory markets, he cut fences, butchered beeves on the ranges—and shot anybody foolish enough to get in his way.

This was the set-up that Bill McDonald found wait-ing for him in the Panhandle, but he let it be known at once that he would stand for no foolishness—that he was in the northwest to do a particular job, and that he intended to see it well done.

He filled the jails, and when the jails were full he locked his prisoners in box cars on the railroad sidings, and when these, in turn, were filled, he tied his prisoners with ropes and put them under guard. Needless to say, he used his gun—and some men didn't go to jail at all. And so, in time, it became the boast of Panhandle bad men that some day they intended to drop down to Quanah and "get Bill McDonald." But for some reason or other most men who made threats never seemed to get around to the business.

But one man tried—John Pierce Matthews, sheriff of Childress County—and Sheriff Matthews died. It occurred like this—

Matthews, who already had two notches on his gun handle, first became an enemy of McDonald when refused admittance to a secret order which McDonald headed in Wichita Falls long before Matthews had attained the badge of sheriff. Thus it was that when McDonald came to live at Quanah in Hardeman County, Matthews, who visited the place frequently, was always glad to find an excuse for renewing the charges that Captain Bill had caused his "black-balling."

Matthews, in the adjoining county, began pistol practice, sometimes boasting to friends that he would wipe out his enemy some day. Quite often the two enemies met on the streets of Quanah, but nothing happened. Then, one evening found Matthews in a belligerent mood as he made a call in the Hardeman capital, and he decided that the time was ripe to kill the Ranger captain.

He called three cronies, including Sheriff Dick Coffer of Hardeman, placed a plug of chewing tobacco and a notebook in the left breast pocket of his coat, and went forth to find the Ranger, after sending word to the latter that he was ready to patch up old difficulties.

They met on a street corner—one Ranger against four men. McDonald opened the conversation.

"I understand you are going to wipe up the earth with me," he said. "What about it?"

"No," said Matthews, with a string of good Texas oaths, "I didn't say that, but I'll tell you what I did say"—and dodging behind Coffer he drew and opened fire on the Ranger . . . the first bullet cutting through McDonald's coat collar.

Captain Bill already had his gun out, but he couldn't fire for fear of hitting Coffer, but he did manage to step around the Hardeman sheriff and let go two shots at Matthews—both striking the man's left breast pocket! The tobacco and the notebook saved Matthews and allowed him to get in another shot, which entered the captain's left shoulder and lodged in the small of his back.

McDonald staggered, but as Matthews fired again he was able to brush the pistol barrel aside. The bullet passed through the Ranger's hat brim. Coffer, meantime, had dropped to the ground and opened fire, putting two bullets through the Ranger's left arm. But McDonald, just as another bullet struck him in the neck, pulled the trigger again and Matthews fell, his three friends taking flight.

The captain was still on his feet, and now he edged himself to a post and slipped down to the ground. His fingers were paralyzed and he told the gathering crowd that he felt like a "dead rabbit." But he wasn't. Bill McDonald, with four wounds in his body, lived, and after two months was up again and back on duty.

Matthews lasted a week, but before he died he sent word to the Ranger that "I'm sorry I can't see you and apologize."

The stories that surround the career of this famous "captain courageous" are too numerous to recount here, but until his death a few years ago he carried a medal presented to him by Fort Worth citizens for running down two hold-up men he stumbled onto while boarding a train for Wichita Falls.

As he stood on the car steps he noticed two men edge up to an old gentleman on the platform and heard a moment later, the old man's cries of "thief!" McDonald acted quickly. He caught one of the hold-up men red-handed, turned him over to station employes and went in pursuit of the other.

The chase ended when the fugitive entered a house on Commerce Street. McDonald went in after him and, pushing aside the curtain over the door of one room, found the man ready to hurl a bottle of acid. The captain drew and fired, the bullet scraping the fugitive's arm. After that it was easy. The arrest was made, and a few weeks later McDonald received a gold medal from

Fort Worth citizens for his ability as a man-catcher . . . and a sprinter.

Governor Hogg and Adjutant General W. S. Mabry put thumbs down on an adventure which promised to be one of the officer's greatest.

Visiting Mexico City to bring back a bank embezzler, Captain McDonald met President Porfirio Diaz, who was engaged in a small war at the time with Guatemala. Discussing the situation, McDonald told the president frankly that he didn't admire the Mexican soldiers, adding that he could take a company of Texas Rangers, go down to Guatemala and win the war in a day's time.

The President remarked that although he had always admired the Rangers, he had to remember that they had killed a great many Mexicans.

"But only the kind that needed killing," the captain interrupted—and Diaz agreed.

It was then that Don Porfirio proposed that McDonald enlist a company of Texans to fight the Guatemalan war and win it. The captain put the matter up to the governor and the adjutant, but they refused to give him leave.

It was Captain McDonald who settled the difficulty when, in 1906, negro soldiers from the Twenty-first Infantry at Fort Brown rioted in Brownsville and committed a murder. When the command at the fort failed to find the guilty men and punish them a Brownsville citizens' committee asked the governor for Rangers. McDonald went, and with him his sergeant, W. J. McCauley.

The citizens warned them that if they went to the

fort to investigate they probably would be shot by negro sentries, but that didn't stop the pair. They walked through the gates and, by using double-barreled shotguns as persuaders, passed the' sentries. And when they came out again they had the men they wanted—and had booked two white officers as accessories before and after the fact.

Bill McDonald, though the best of the riot breakers, was more than that. He broke up a dozen lynching mobs, almost single-handed; he rounded up the Buzzard Water Hole gang of thieves and killers on the San Saba; he put the quietus on many a Texas family feud; he solved a dozen bank robbery and murder cases—but, above all, he set a new style of social conduct in the Panhandle.

It was this latter accomplishment which caused a former district attorney in the Panhandle to say to Colonel E. M. House, in a letter:

"History should hand down his name for the coming generations by the side of the heroes of the Alamo and San Jacinto."

One Ranger, one riot. Bill McDonald wasn't the only one.

When, in the Spring of 1907, trouble threatened in Trinity County over a local option election, Ranger James D. Dunaway was sent to Grovetown to watch the situation.

Both the wet and dry factions resented the intrusion of an outsider in local affairs and, though it is uncertain who started it, Ranger Dunaway and County Attorney

Robb, while crossing a street, were caught by a heavy volley of revolver shots.

Mr. Robb was fatally wounded and the Ranger went down with seventeen wounds. Dunaway was carried into a grocery store and given first aid. While waiting for a physician, the man with seventeen wounds said to a bystander: "I guess I'd better report this to the governor."

He called for pencil and paper and this is the telegram he wrote to Governor T. M. Campbell:

"Shot all to pieces, but not serious."

CHAPTER XVIII

Five Hundred Steers for a Ranger's Head

A BANDIT GANG on the Mexican bank of the Río Grande wanted a man's head—and as a price they were ready to pay five hundred head of steers to get it.

But in the end they had to keep their livestock, because Captain J. Monroe Fox of the Texas Rangers had but one head, and he had no intention of giving it for his country. There was, however, some temptation, for when the posting of the reward became known in the Big Bend country of Texas, Captain Fox, with a grin on the side of his face, promptly sent word to the bold banditti that he might talk business if they would first agree to deliver the cattle to the American side of the river.

And then he laughed and went on with the day's work—which had to do, principally, with making life miserable for the gentlemen who had offered the reward.

"It finally turned out that we got some of *their* heads," said the captain, as he hoisted a stein of beer in an Austin café. He put down his glass and pushed back the brim of his broad Stetson hat. "And when we didn't get 'em," he added, "Pancho Villa did.'

The veteran Texas officer, who first joined up with the Rangers in 1911 to work ten years in the dangerous border service, has only a good word for the Scourge of the Chihuahua desert.

"The best friend the Rangers ever had on the Río

165

Grande, old Pancho . . . why, he's executed many a bad 'un for me!" And that reminded the captain of a story from out his own experiences—a story of gunfire, murder and sudden death, followed by Ranger justice, swift and sure.

It was early in the year 1915 at Fabens, El Paso County, and on a dark street of the town. Rangers Lee Burdett and Charles Bell were chasing three Mexicans suspected of thievery. They had caught one and while Burdett pointed the barrel of a six-shooter at the fugitive's heart, Bell went through the man's pockets. But even as they were engaged in the search there was a sudden spurt of fire from behind a near-by fence and Burdett fell, a bullet through his neck. As the slug struck, however, he squeezed convulsively on the trigger of his own revolver and the Mexican before him toppled over, shot squarely through the heart.

Ranger Bell whirled, and a chunk of lead whanged by his own head, embedding itself in a house wall. Bell caught a momentary glimpse of two shadowy figures in the dark and opened up with his six-shooter. There was a brief exchange of shots and then the two killers fled into the night, running in the direction of the border.

Ranger Bell bent over his companion . . . Burdett was dead.

Captain Fox was at headquarters in Marfa when the news reached his ears, and, since there is a sort of unwritten law in the Rangers that no time must be lost in avenging a comrade's death, the captain went to work at once.

Across the Río Grande near the scene of the killing

was a battalion of Villista troops under command of one Colonel Talimenta, and Captain Fox contacted the Colonel for an immediate conference.

"One of my Rangers has been killed," Fox informed him, "and since the murderers escaped to your side of the river, something must be done about it."

The Colonel shrugged his shoulders.

"But they weren't my men," he said, "so what can I do about it?"

"You can find out who they were," suggested the Ranger, "and if you'll do that . . . and if you'll catch 'em . . . well, would $150 be enough . . . just for delivery to me?"

"Impossible!" exclaimed Talimenta. "I have no authority to catch men on this side and turn them over to Texans—but I'll do this for you . . . I'll find the men, if I can, and have them put against the wall. Would that be satisfactory?"

Captain Fox said that it would and he went back across the river to wait for news from Talimenta.

A week passed, and no word came. The Ranger captain grew restless with the delay, and he went again to see the colonel.

"Yes," admitted the officer, "I have learned who they were, but . . the men of my command won't stand for an execution. So I am powerless. What can I do? señor?" Again he shrugged his shoulders.

Fox said little, but when he went back to the Texas side he told his men that he was going to El Paso, and thence across to Juárez. If the Colonel would do nothing, perhaps the General would, for Pancho Villa wasn't the kind to be bossed by the men of his command.

"When I arrived at Villista headquarters in Juárez," recalled Fox, "I went in to see Villa immediately. The big Mexican listened in silence while I explained the situation and then said: 'Talimenta's men may dictate to him; it's different here. I'll find the killers and arrange for you to witness the execution.'"

And Pancho Villa was as good as his word. Captain Fox was back in Marfa when the word came over to El Paso that the slayers of Burdett had been found. Villista headquarters asked if the Rangers cared to have a man present as the firing squad did its work. Doctor Goodwin, Ranger medical officer in El Paso at the time, accepted the invitation and crossed to Juárez. There he met Villista officers and with them rode to the outskirts of the city, where the firing squad was drawn up and waiting.

It was brief business. The two men were stood at the roadside while the squad of riflemen were lined up across from them. An officer raised a sword, and dropped its point; and eight spurts of fire darted across the road . . . Ranger Lee Burdett was avenged.

The captain of the execution party collected the empty rifle cartridges and gave them to Dr. Goodwin. Later, Captain Fox carried the shells to Burdett's mother in Austin, but she didn't care to keep the grim mementos.

So it went in those days—

The raiding wasn't so intense and vicious and well-organized as it had been in the days of Captains Mc-

Nelly and Hughes. Only small independent bands were coming over, the bloody lusty among the bold caballeros finding plenty of outlet for their emotions by joining such organizations as those led by Villa and Zapata. Mexico was in the throes of revolt, the tide of battle sweeping southward toward the City of Mexico, and so most potential border bandits were slinging carbines with the various troops.

The Ranger force, however, had plenty of watchful duty to do after Villa had returned from the capture of Mexico City, and the New Mexican town of Columbus had been sacked . . . for the ammunition smugglers were as busy as bees along the border about that time. In connection with the raid on Columbus, though, Captain Fox is one of Pancho's staunchest supporters. Contrary to claims made in recent magazine articles, the Captain is firm in his belief that Villa took no part, personally, in the Columbus affair.

"Because the night before the raid I was in El Paso and one of Villa's own men showed me a note that proved, to my own satisfaction, that the general was deep down in Chihuahua at the time," said Fox. "And the note was in Pancho's own writing, which I knew well. He said that he had been sick, that he had been on a hunting trip, and that he would be ready to ride again within ten days. But, anyhow, he got the blame for the raid."

Perry M. Ross, Fort Worth newspaperman, verifies that statement. In March of 1916 Ross was with Villa on a deer hunt at Rancho Bustillos for five days before and five days after the Columbus fight. Rancho

Bustillos is about three hundred and fifty miles south of the border.

"Antonio (Red) Lopez, a former lieutenant who had broken with Villa, was the leader at Columbus," says Ross, "and even before that time Pancho had posted a reward of fifty thousand pesos for Red's head. It was in revenge for this that Lopez caused his men to raise the shout of 'Viva Villa!' as they rode into the town. Villa later executed Red Lopez at Chihuahua City."

Captain Fox states that the general himself later assured him that he had no part in the affair, which brought on General Pershing's immediate invasion of the Southern Republic.

But even with the wars raging over the line, life wasn't exactly a peaceful siesta for the Rangers on Río Grande duty.

For Señor Chico Cano was doing his very best to turn the American side into a happy hunting ground just then, keeping the Rangers more or less busy pumping the levers of their Winchesters. Chico was the biggest of the big bad men in the current crop of banditti and he tried time and again to lead the Texans into traps.

He succeeded once, and killed two of Captain Fox's best men—Ranger Eugene Hulen, a brother of Brigadier General John Hulen of Fort Worth, and Joe Sitter, one of the best man-trackers in the organization.

In May of 1915 Chico Cano and his band of thieves crossed the line in Jeff Davis County on a livestock lifting expedition, but after they came over they evidently decided they had rather kill Rangers than steal cattle. Knowing that the Fox company was in the vicinity, they laid a trap and made a trail that the victims might find and follow.

The crossing was reported, as the bandits hoped it might be, and five Rangers rode at once for the river . . . H. C. Trollinger, Soup Cummings, Charles Craighead, Hulen and Sitter.

They went first to the house of an old Mexican, near the scene of the crossing, to make inquiries and they learned from the occupant that Chico's men, even then, were hiding out a few miles down the river. The Ranger detachment set off in the direction indicated, all unaware that another Mexican had overheard the conversation and had sent a boy downstream to warn Cano.

Sitter, whose reputation as a trailer had become almost legendary, wasn't long in finding the scent, which led to a box canyon in between two hills on the American side. Here the Texans stopped and considered a plan of action. Maybe the raiders had moved on—but if they hadn't, this canyon likely was a trap. Sitter and Hulen finally decided to take a chance. They would take the lead, skirt up the left side of the canyon to see what they could see and then, if nothing happened, the other three could follow up the right side.

Sitter and Hulen rode away—to a rendezvous with death. They had not gone far up the valley before a blaze of rifle fire roared from the rims above. Chico Cano and his men had set a good trap. They had waited on the heights to pour down a deadly rain of bullets as the two rode in. One burst of fire and . . . Ranger Hulen nevermore would ride the border . . . Ranger Sitter would follow no more trails. Trollinger, Cummings and Craighead heard the firing and rode forward to join the mêlée, but another volley forced them to dismount and take cover in the brush. They fired back, but the Mexicans were too well hidden in the foliage on the rim for them to get in a telling shot. For awhile they exchanged shot for shot, and then, seeing that they were hopelessly outnumbered and in a trap, they fell back to get reinforcements. Their horses, during the firing, had taken flight, and so they went on foot to bring back other members of the company.

The Mexicans were gone when Captain Fox and his Rangers arrived at the canyon, but they found Hulen and Sitter where they had fallen.

Captain Fox bided his time and at last he evened up the count—in January of the following year.

Accompanied by six ranchers, the captain and eight men of his command jumped a raiding party in practically the same general locality—on the American side across from Candelaria—but this time it was the Texans who were on the outside of the corner.

"We got them where they couldn't get away, and then we just lay behind a few little knolls and played a waiting game," said Captain Fox. "We'd wait for a bandit to reveal his position and then we'd let him have it. Only a few of the gang escaped . . . for when the scrap was over we found sixteen bodies in the brush.

"How did we know it was the same gang that killed Hulen and Sitter? Well, we found on one of the bodies a watch that Trollinger had dropped during the other fight; and on one of the captured horses we found Trollinger's saddle, stolen after the other raid."

Over the killing of those sixteen a great cry went up from the Mexican population in the districts of Candelaria and Parvenier, Fox recalls, and there was an investigation, but it ended in justification for the Rangers and the ranchers.

Sometimes, during those days along the border, a little humor was mixed in with the tragedy. Once a band of eighty Mexicans, after crossing into Brewster County to burn several stores and kill a four-year-old boy, departed for Mexico with seven Americans and a negro as their prisoners. The Rangers arrived at the scene and were preparing to cross the Río Grande for a pursuit when they saw a party of men approaching the river from the Mexican interior. The prisoners were coming home. They said that the Mexicans had attempted to haul them to the interior in a truck stolen at a mine, but that a tire had gone flat after a few miles' ride. The main raiding party had ridden on, leaving only five men to guard the captives, but while tire repairs were being made the guards became so interested in the business that the prisoners were able to overpower them and make an escape.

The captain looks back on his service with the Rangers as the most interesting phase of his long career in law enforcement. In the '90s he served the city of Austin as constable and detective, and before he entered the state service under Governor Colquitt he had been a city detective in Houston. Then, later, after leaving the Rangers he had guarded oil company payrolls around Tampico; was chief of police at Corpus Christi and at Brownwood.

"All good jobs, but give me the Ranger service every time," says he. "But listen . . . did I ever tell you about the time that General Aniceto Pizano and sixty-one men crossed the border with an idea of taking Texas back for Mexico. Well, that's another story . . . "

CAPTAIN J. MONROE FOX

CHAPTER XIX

Aniceto Pizano Dreams a Dream

ANICETO PIZANO had a dream—but when he awoke to a realization of the things-that-are it had turned into a nightmare.

And the Texas Rangers were the bogies in the background.

Don Aniceto's dream was one that many another, and more famous, generalissimo had dreamed before him—but if such genius as that possessed by Napoleon, Frederick the Great and Cæsar had failed to make it work, what could be expected of a half-pint Mexican general who took his inspiration from the neck of a mescal bottle?

But none could say that Pizano was not ambitious, for no man lacking in ambition, and in patriotism, would have set out to do the thing he attempted . . . recapture and annexation of the state of Texas for the Republic of Mexico! A laudable and noble ambition, but sixty-one men were not many for such an enterprise.

Early in 1915 Señor Pizano was wholly unknown to fame, being at that time a somewhat minor military man with headquarters in and about the city of Matamoras. He wasn't even a general—but along sometime in the spring, that season when the thoughts of men are supposed to turn to romantic possibilities, Don Aniceto became visionary. He looked across the Texas border and thought of many things—of how the Texans, back in

'36 had wrested this rich land from the mother country; of General Woll's invasion in the '40s; and of the intermittent warfare that had raged along the border since.

And then he had the Big Idea.

He would raise a force, a group of bold *caballeros* who feared neither death nor the devil . . . nor the Texas Rangers. And then he would strike, with a quick lightning-like thrust that would carry him over the border and through the ranchlands . . . to San Antonio, and then to Austin; and when those two cities had been twisted to his will he would move on to the conquest of other regions.

"And then, with Texas under my thumb," he told himself, "I'll move on and take in New Mexico and later, perhaps, Southern California."

Pizano smiled. He assured himself that he was a great man; in fact, a genius; and from that moment on he became *El General*, the self-appointed *jefe* of a conquering army. It was just as well; for he was tired of doing guard duty on the Mexican Central railroad.

But there was one fly in the ointment. He had no army. So he sewed on some shoulder straps, procured for himself a large sword, buckled the same around his waist, and went forth to muster a regiment. He had rare good luck and within a month sixty-one men, all armed to the teeth and ready for a fight, were on the rolls. Perhaps he might have enlisted more, but after looking over his aggregation—with their heavy rifles, well-oiled revolvers and well-filled bandoliers—he decided that he had enough.

Early in August, General Pizano prepared to strike,

but he didn't tell the Mexican government anything
about his plans—he was saving that as a surprise after
the capture of Texas and New Mexico. He and his
irregulars would show the world a thing or two.

They mounted their horses, set their straw sombreros
at a jaunty angle and crossed the Río Grande near San
Benito, ready to strike the first blow at Norris Ranch,
thirty miles to the north.

But a party of sixty-one men can't ride abroad without some notice being taken, and their presence on the
American side was reported almost immediately to
Ranger forces and to the Adjutant General's office in
Austin. Thus Adjutant General Henry Hutchings (who
incidentally holds that office at the present time) heard
the news about the hour that Pizano forces arrived at
the Norris Ranch. He immediately put messages on the
wires instructing Captain Henry Ransom and Captain
J. Monroe Fox to start at once for the rancho; Ransom
from Brownsville with ten men and Fox from Marfa
with eighteen; and then the Adjutant himself, and a
few rangers from headquarters, left Austin for the
scene.

The Ranger companies threw their saddles on special
trains and started, the captains wiring ahead and
instructing the Norris Ranch foreman to have horses
ready for a quick ride; but when the Rangers arrived
they discovered that things already had been occurring
at the ranch. General Pizano had ridden in and shot up
the place, but had retired. He considered the raid a
victory, however, because he had succeeded in capturing
eight head of horses.

The Rangers found mounts ready and waiting. They saddled, and then held a council of war. Word had been received that the invaders had been seen a few miles to the south and General Hutchings was for riding in that direction in quest of the party, and away they went— for a fifteen-mile canter through the morning. But they didn't find *El General* Pizano and his army.

"I have an idea that the best thing to do would be a double back to the ranch," suggested Captain Fox. "They may attempt to return and make another raid."

They rode back to the Norris place—and ran squarely into a fight. General Pizano *had* decided to double on his track. It didn't last long, that fight under the late afternoon sun . . . for a few volleys from the rifles of the Rangers gave the "unconquerables" the hint to turn tail and run for it, and as they disappeared over the horizon the Rangers started out to take stock of damage done.

"Frank Hamer (later a captain) was a member of my company then," said Captain Fox, "and Hamer and I visited some of the Mexican houses to see if anybody had been hurt. In a dark room of one shack we stumbled over the body of a dead Mexican woman, and in the road outside we found a horribly wounded Mexican man. Only one American had been hurt, a ranch hand named Martin."

At daylight next morning the Rangers took up the trail—which led southward, the *muy valiente* Pizano having decided that foreign invasion was not the bread-and-milk sort of business he had first dreamed of. A few miles to the south Fox and his men found one of

Pizano's irregulars lying beside the road, the top of his head blown away, and the face powder-burned. He had, too, a rifle wound in the body, indicating that when he had fallen wounded from his horse one of the irregulars had reined in long enough to give him the silencing ceremony of the *coup de grace*. Dead men tell no tales.

From that point started the great race for the Río Grande, with Pizano's army in front and the Rangers following close in the rear; close enough at times to halt for a moment, get in a few spurts of rifle fire, then take up the tiring chase once more; and in that running fight of thirty miles many a Mexican saddle was emptied by a bullet.

For two years after skeletons were discovered along the route of battle . . . where some wounded irregular had crawled away to die.

Once on the mad flight the invaders tried to raise the flag of truce, a white rag on a pole, but pulled it in when they saw that the Texans were not vastly interested.

And so, El General Aniceto Pizano, a sadder but a wiser man, recrossed the Río Grande, and he was glad to be home again. His dream of conquest, fame and power had turned into a nightmare—with the Texas Rangers playing the rôle of the "bogey" man.

And his ten men also were glad to be home again. Ten men?

Ten out of sixty-one?

"Yes," said Captain Fox, "I think that figure's right . . . we didn't get them all, you know."

Captain Tom Hickman. *Photo courtesy of the Texas Ranger Hall of Fame and Museum, Waco, Texas.*

CHAPTER XX

Captain Hickman Wields "The Broom"

HE WAS an impressive looking gent—as impressive as a checkered suit, a jaunty cap, a pair of spats, and a set of horn-rimmed spectacles could make him; and when he rapped discreetly at the door of the Elite gambling hall in Longview, the lookout took one glance and let him in.

Here was a man with money to spend. The elegance of his clothes fairly screamed the message—a tenderfoot from the East, a certain and easy mark for the gentlemen who presided at the roulette wheel and behind the poker tables. Who else but an Easterner would be wearing spats and a checkered suit in the rip-roaring East Texas oil boom town that was Longview in the fall of 1930.

The lookout man scrutinized the stranger, sized him up . . . perhaps one of the lease hounds or royalty buyers who had been flooding the town since the lure of black gold had reached out to the far corners of the nation to bring a cosmopolitan swarm into the greatest oil field in the world. The lookout man let the dandy pass; not only that—he ousted one of the habitues from his chair at the poker table that the effete visitor might have a place to sit and try his luck.

But the stranger didn't sit. Instead—

"I'm Captain Tom Hickman of the Texas Rangers," he said, "and I'm here to close this place."

181

There was a sudden silence in the place. The click of poker chips ceased; the whirr of the roulette wheel was stilled; all eyes were on the gent in the checkered suit and the fawn-colored spats—and then somebody laughed.

"You a Ranger!" exclaimed this individual, a man who sat behind the poker table riffling a deck of cards in his fingers. "You a Ranger! That's a laugh!"

And the other gamblers in the room must have agreed, for a gale of merriment rippled over the place. They looked again at the stranger; he didn't wear high-heeled boots, and he didn't wear a tall hat.

"You'll have to show us, brother," someone said. "We've seen Rangers before and we know what they look like. Where's your authority?"

The Captain said he would be glad to accommodate. From an inside coat pocket he took his commission and his badge and displayed it before the eyes of the proprietor, but some still were skeptical, even though they had glimpsed the pearl handles of two .45 Colt revolvers under the checkered coat.

"Well, in that case," said Hickman, "maybe these three gentlemen can identify me." He pointed out three men, apparently oil field roustabouts, who stood at the edge of the crowd, each grinning behind a two-days' growth of beard. "Let me introduce some of the boys," he added, "Stewart Stanley, Hale Kirby and A. B. Hamm, all members of Company B of the Texas Rangers . . . they've been with you for an hour or so."

That's why half a hundred gamblers paid fines at Longview's city hall that day.

And that's a sample of how Captain Hickman, with headquarters in Fort Worth, "handled the broom" for half a dozen oil field cleanups when the great East Texas area opened the lid for the world's biggest petroleum pool and thus drew to it the riff-raff that follows in the wake of such events. They were not, as a rule, dangerous men, these camp followers—just confidence men, gamblers, bootleggers and narcotic salesmen—but they came in such numbers that local law enforcement agencies were hard put to cope with the situation.

But Captain Hickman and his ten men of Company B didn't take long for the clean-up job. They were impartial; they showed no distinctions; and if a man looked as though he might have a blot on his conscience he went into custody for investigation. They cleaned out Overton and Gladewater, and then went to the third of the mushroom towns, Kilgore. There was no jail in the latter place, at least none large enough to hold the catch, but that didn't give the Rangers pause.

The First Methodist Church at Kilgore had been abandoned, and here the Rangers took their prisoners, lining them in the aisles, clamping the leg and iron chains on a select few who were suspected of major crimes. And when the drive was over, and the "fish" were sorted out, it was discovered that the net had dropped on several men wanted for murder in West Texas counties.

Tom Hickman is one of the most colorful of the modern-day captains. He didn't fight Comanches, and the raiding storm on the Mexican border was spent when he first joined up in 1919, but he typifies as well as any other man, the service of the modern times . . . although he isn't in the Rangers now.

But before Governor "Ma" Ferguson came into office in 1933 to fire Captain Hickman and his entire company—lock, stock and barrel—he put in almost fourteen years of continuous service. Hickman is a native of Cooke County, where he spent his boyhood on his father's farm; but by the time he had grown to young manhood he had grown tired of work behind a span of mules and he put in application for enlistment in the Rangers. Two years later he received his appointment, with orders to report for duty with a company in the Texas Big Bend, that wild and untamed region in the southwest corner of the state which is, if there is one, the last frontier. Here he learned the tricks of his new trade, by arresting bad men, both Mexican and American, and by watching the border against invasion. Within eighteen months he was a captain and his company a mobile force that ranged the state from one corner to another.

"In six years time," says the captain, "I established residence in twenty-three different towns, ranging from Marfa on the border to Sherman in the northeast, and from Wichita Falls in the north to Corpus Christi on the gulf."

He and his men rode a patrol in the longshoresmen's strike in Galveston in 1920; he was in the Panhandle in 1928 when that area became the oil center of the state and the mecca of the lawless element in the Southwest. He helped establish martial law in Borger following the killing of District Attorney John A. Holmes, but to

Captain Hickman the business never was exciting and dangerous.

"We really had little trouble in the oil towns," says the captain, whose modesty almost verges on taciturnity. "The name Texas Ranger, you know, has a lot of weight behind it."

And a lot of tradition and reputation—that's why tough oil towns could be subdued without gunplay, for men saw the big white hat and the tall brown boots and said to themselves: "This is the law of Texas."

Captain Hickman and Ranger Stanley "just happened to be in Clarksville" on the day in 1926 when a bandit gang decided to rob the Red River National Bank. The captain was walking past the building when he caught a glimpse of the robbery taking place behind the window. He rushed to his auto for his rifle, a Remington automatic, and then called to Stanley and two local officers who were talking to Stanley's father near by.

The party, their guns ready, waited outside the bank for two of the holdup men to emerge and join a third who waited in a car outside. The two came out, one carrying a suitcase; and Captain Hickman, who had taken up a position across the street, dropped down on one knee and commanded the pair to halt. Instead the bandits started running, and one drew a pistol.

Captain Hickman opened fire with the automatic rifle, the three other officers joining in. Both bandits dropped, one dead and the other fatally wounded. The tightly-stuffed valise also fell and burst open—to spill $30,000 in currency and silver on the sidewalk as the third man escaped after abandoning his auto.

Thus, death closed an incident which, a short time later, led the Texas Bankers' Association to post a standing five thousand dollar reward for dead bank robbers.

Captain Hickman, while on duty, nearly always wore his two pearl-handled .45 calibre Colt revolvers—not for any "two-gun reason," the Captain explains, but because two are better than one and are much easier and more comfortable to carry. But they fit him well in the rôle he has often been called upon to play as representative Texas Ranger.

They've been seen, those two enormous revolvers, in half of Europe, for he wore them twice when he went abroad—once as rodeo judge for the British Empire Exposition in London in 1924, and once when he went on a tour of Europe with the Simmons University Cowboy band. And on the latter occasion he attracted, as a "live and kicking" Ranger, considerably more attention than the band itself.

He laughs as he recalls how he helped educate the producer of Río Rita on the proper costumes for the Rangers used in that musical production. It was during the. administration of Governor Dan Moody. One morning the governor called the captain to his office and said:

"Tom, I've just returned from New York and while there I saw the show called Río Rita. The clothes worn by the Ranger actors weren't exactly modeled after what I've seen here in Texas. Do you own a tuxedo?"

"No," replied the captain, "but I have a dress suit . . . why?"

"Well," explained the governor, "I want you to drag out that dress suit, put it on and have your picture made. I want to show the producers of Rio Rita how a real Texas Ranger dresses."

And the captain did have the picture made, and the governor did send it to the producers in New York. The two famous guns weren't in evidence—unless they were hidden under the swallow tails.

Captain Hickman and his ten men, some of whom had service records almost as long as Hickman himself, found themselves in the discard when the woman governor moved into the statehouse in January of 1933, but the big six-foot officer who is in his forties and whose wide grin has become one of the most famous in the state, didn't kick about it. He isn't built that way. He merely smiled and observed that "orders are orders."

Today he still is working for the state—a tax supervisor in charge of beer revenue work in North Texas—but the former Rangers of his old company who drop in from time to time at the old Ranger headquarters at 425 South Adams Street in Fort Worth still call the place "headquarters," especially the Captain's room, where the walls are decorated with quirts, lariat ropes, saddles and other service equipment. He still wears the big white hat and the high-heeled boots of the cowboy—and he plays polo for a thrill.

His hair is turning a bit gray about the edges, but his deep-set black eyes mirror the calmness and the imperturbability for which he is noted under all and any circumstances.

"Think you're tough, don't you?" a gambling game impressario growled as the Captain swung an axe into a dice table in a downtown Fort Worth hotel.

Tom Hickman merely flashed his famous grin and went on with his hacking.

"Nope," he said, "not tough . . . just rough."

Captain Frank Hamer. *Photo courtesy of the Texas Ranger Hall of Fame and Museum, Waco, Texas.*

CHAPTER XXI

The Rangers Versus Gangland

THE Texas Ranger, in turning back the edges of a great frontier, gave the Comanche extra arrows and beat him on his native field; he allowed the bandit of the Border what tolerance that he could, then booted him across the Río Grande; but there came at last one enemy that he could not combat—the long, far-reaching arm of politics.

On that January day, in 1933, when Miriam A. Ferguson went up to the statehouse in Austin to take for the second time the oath as governor of Texas, the old-time members of the Ranger force, from headquarters company to the posts afield, began gathering up their kits and looking about for other jobs to do.

These men—most of them trained man-hunters with service records running from ten to thirty years—already had sensed the direction of the political wind, already knew that the end was near; and, before nightfall, forecast had become reality.

With a few strokes of the pen Governor "Ma" Ferguson and her husband Jim proved that that implement sometimes can be more powerful than the sword . . . for they succeeded, during the brief space of one day, in wrecking an organization whose traditions had been in the making through almost a hundred years of Texas history.

Some of the older officers—men like Captain Frank

Hamer, with twenty-seven years of service to his credit —didn't even wait for the notice from the quartermaster. They preferred to resign and call the matter closed.

"Besides," said Captain Hamer, bullet-scarred veteran of half a hundred encounters, "it is better not to be commanded by a woman."

The big six-footer, who had learned his lessons under the tutelage of Captain J. H. Rogers, retired to his home in Austin to enter private criminology and to watch in silence, like his former companions, the work of the younger men who came to fill the Ranger roster. Francis Augustine Hamer was scarcely more than a boy when he first entered the Ranger service—down in the Big Bend after Captain Rogers had seen the blue-eyed young giant, a former blacksmith, subdue a fighting tough and handcuff him to a windmill. And in the years which followed he gained a reputation for fearlessness and expert marksmanship as he helped the Rogers company preserve the peace along the border.

But even today he refuses to discuss the incidents of his career along the international line, events which included a part in the defeat of Aniceto Pizano, when that ambitious Mexican general invaded Texas with the idea of conquest.

He was a captain, in 1927, when two Mexicans were put on "the spot" outside a Stanton bank by persons plotting to collect the $5,000 reward the Texas Bankers Association was offering at the time for each dead bank bandit. Hamer solved the case and one killer received the death penalty.

He was in charge at Borger, in 1929, when that Pan-handle city, filled with the riff-raff followers of oil booms, required the attention of state Rangers. He directed the work of driving the criminal element from the town and helped solve the murder of District Attorney John A. Holmes, who had been blown to bits by nitroglycerin when he refused to obey the mandates of the underworld.

At Sherman, in 1930, he stood on the steps of the courthouse and defied a mob of howling citizens who threatened to enter and take a negro prisoner charged with assault of a white woman.

"Come on up if you feel lucky," he shouted, "but if you try it there'll be a lot of funerals in Sherman to-night." The mob didn't try.

These were mere instances. Scores of other encounters were on his brilliant record of long service but now, with a new administration coming into office, Captain Hamer, at the age of fifty, found himself relegated to the sidelines.

The early months of 1933 slipped by . . . and then something occurred which was to arouse the indignation of every law-abiding Texan, and which, in the end, was to bring back into the spotlight the old-type Ranger and his method of doing business. It came in the form of a one-man crime wave, carried out by a former Dallas chicken thief who had risen from a petty hood-lum to a killer more merciless and vicious than the deadly John Wesley Hardin.

But Clyde Barrow could hardly be placed in the same category with the iniquitous John, whose blazing .41s snuffed out so many lives before the Rangers ran him down in the '70s. John Wesley had something of a code of honor; the modern gangster product of a West Dallas theft ring had none.

"He was just a wild-eyed kid when the fellows first brought him to the hangout and said he was all right," a captured member of his old gang recalled. "And I remember when he took part in his first holdup . . . it was in the Big Bend and he carried a Saturday night gun which wouldn't shoot. He said then that some day he intended to have some good, big guns that would shoot."

Subsequent events show how well he succeeded.

Paroled in 1932 from the Texas prison, where he had been sent for burglary in McLennan County, the former chicken thief launched immediately one of the bloodiest crime careers since the days of Billy the Kid.

At midnight of April 27, 1932, in the central Texas town of Hillsboro, one John Bucher, a merchant, surprised a prowler robbing his store. A flash of flame, the roar of a pistol . . . and Bucher lay dead on the floor.

The saga of Clyde Barrow had begun.

It was the start of a murderous trail that twisted from Iowa to the Gulf, a trail lined with looted banks and dead men in the road—men shot down by a killer who moved across the country in a fast car, continually doubling on his own tracks and making five hundred mile jumps in a single night.

Barrow had acquired the "good, big guns" he wanted.

August, 1932—A sheriff and his deputy at Atoka,

Oklahoma, saw a man lift a bottle to his lips in a dance hall. "You can't do that!" shouted the sheriff. "I can't, can't I?" came the reply, accompanied by a burst of gunfire. Undersheriff Eugene Moore fell dead, the sheriff wounded. Witnesses identified Clyde Barrow as the man who fled.

August, 1932—Howard Hall, an aged merchant of Sherman, Texas, looked into the muzzle of a bandit's gun. He resisted and went down from a blow of the robber's weapon. He died as three shots were drilled into his prostrate form. Sherman police hunted Clyde Barrow.

December, 1932—In Temple, Texas, Doyle Johnson found a man attempting to steal his car. He protested, a pistol flashed. Barrow took the car, and earned another murder charge.

January, 1933—Officers were met with gunfire as they raided a Dallas home suspected of harboring criminals. Deputy Sheriff Malcolm Davis of Tarrant County died in the front yard. The chicken thief was progressing . . .

April, 1933—Raiders approached a house in Joplin, Missouri. From a window a machine gun rattled . . . Detective Harry McGinnis and Constable Wes Harryman fell dead, riddled with bullets. And no more was heard of Clyde Barrow until—

June, 1933—He appeared in Alma, Arkansas, and Officer H. D. Humphrey tried to arrest him. Officer Humphrey died.

Meantime, the Dallas gangster had found a companion —a slender, auburn-haired girl he had known when both were kids over on the west side. Bonnie Parker was twenty years old and attractive. She had a job as waitress in a café but she didn't particularly enjoy the work. Life behind the counter was too dull and monotonous. She preferred something more zestful, more adventuresome, than carrying out food to casual customers. And besides, she was rather lonely, with her husband serving time in the Texas prison for burglary. Consequently, it didn't take her long to decide when Clyde Barrow proposed that she join him on his forays over the country. She became, in fact, his light o' love, riding with him in his heavily-armed auto, covering with a sawed-off shotgun his retreats from plundred banks. She became, in time, as expert with Clyde's big guns as the outlaw himself, and she gloried in it. She had photographs made of herself in various poses with various weapons. She wanted the world to know that Clyde Barrow's girl was tough . . . she smoked cigars.

One crime excursion after another followed, and as if these weren't thrilling enough, they planned one of the greatest coups of all.

On January 16, 1934, they raided the Eastham State Prison Farm, laid down a machine gun barrage as the convict squads labored in the fields and effected the escape of five prisoners, including one of Barrow's best friends, one Raymond Hamilton, long-term bank robbery convict. A guard, Major Crowson, was killed in the mêlée.

The incident served to intensify the hunt for the outlaw and the girl who rode beside him. They were reported in various sections of the country and, although trap after trap was set by the state's various law enforcement agencies, the quarry always managed to escape.

But Lee Simmons, manager of the state prison system, was determined to avenge the death of Major Crowson. He went to Austin, conferred with the governor, the adjutant general and other executives, and explained a plan he had formulated. He would hire a man to do the job he wanted done, a man to work as an employee of the prison system for the sole purpose of snaring Clyde Barrow, and he said he had in mind one especially qualified for the work in hand.

"I want Frank Hamer," said Manager Simmons and so, on February 10 the captain was called from retirement and hired by the prison system . . . to match old-time Ranger cunning with the shrewdness of the modern gangster.

Hamer went to work—in secret—but even as he worked Barrow and Bonnie struck again.

On Easter Sunday, State Highway Patrolmen E. B. Wheeler and H. D. Murphy turned their motorcycles down a country lane near the North Texas city of Grapevine. A car was parked in the lane—perhaps some motorists in trouble. But as Wheeler and Murphy approached the spot the occupants of the machine, a man and a woman, stepped to the rear of the car and opened fire with automatic shotguns. Wheeler and Murphy—the latter riding his first patrol—were shot from their motorcycles, the flaps of their pistol holsters still unbuttoned. And then, as they lay dead in the road the woman approached one of the bodies, turned it over with her foot, and riddled it with three charges of buckshot.

This, according to William Schieffer, a farmer who witnessed the tragedy and saw the car speed away.

Investigators found an empty whisky bottle at the scene. It bore the fingerprints of Clyde Barrow.

Every road leading out of Texas into adjoining states was watched, but in vain. Several days passed, and then an auto became bogged in the mud ouside the town of Commerce, in northeastern Oklahoma. Commerce officers went to investigate and Constable C. Campbell died with a rifle bullet through his chest. Barrow and Bonnie kidnaped another officer and dashed for Kansas, where they released him after carefully explaining that they had no part in the Grapevine murder.

Meanwhile, Captain Hamer had taken as his chief aide another veteran ex-Ranger who had been employed by Chief L. H. Phares of the Texas Highway Patrol. Hamer and Mannie Gault had but one order—"Get Clyde Barrow"—and to that end they started the tedious task of contacting relatives of the outlaws, and visiting relatives of convicts who had been friends of the pair.

For weeks they followed various clues over all the states of the Southwest, and then turned their attention to Bienville Parish, Louisiana.

"Barrow," Captain Hamer explained later, "was wanted in Texas, Oklahoma, New Mexico, Arkansas, Kansas, Missouri and Iowa because of the long trail of murder he and Bonnie had spread over those states. Louisiana was the one spot where he wasn't 'hot.' And besides, the father of Henry Methvin, one of the men freed in the Eastham farm raid, lived about thirty miles from Arcadia, Louisiana.

"All known relatives of all the crooks Barrow had associated with were watched. We hoped Barrow would visit some of them, and many times we were close on his trail. Several times his meals had hardly been eaten before I got wind of him."

And then Captain Hamer, through a source he refused to divulge, received word that Clyde and Bonnie were about to visit the Methvin home. He mustered help—Deputy Sheriffs Ted Hinton and Bob Alcorn of Dallas—and the four sought the co-operation of Henderson Jordan, the sheriff of Arcadia. The group conferred, framed a trap.

"I am sorry I can't explain exactly how we were certain we would catch them when we did," said Captain Hamer, but anyhow—

On the evening of May 22, 1934, the former Ranger captain received definite information through an informer that the gangster and his girl would drive next morning along a road between Sailes and Gibsland.

Hamer, Gault, the two Dallas deputies and two Louisiana officers drove out on the road indicated, and Hamer selected a spot where the highway, cutting through the piney woods, rose to a slight elevation. He spaced his men at intervals in a ditch at one side of the road and there they waited throughout the night, high-powered automatic rifles resting across their knees.

Dawn flushed the sky and the sun rose, but still Barrow did not come. Seven o'clock, eight, nine . . . the officers were growing tired of the vigil. But Captain

Hamer said that he had confidence in his information. They would hang on awhile longer.

And then, at 9:30, a car was seen approaching from the eastward. It moved along at about forty miles an hour, a leisurely pace if Barrow sat behind the wheel. A truck, coming from the other direction, passed the ambuscade, met the Ford sedan and caused it, momentarily, to slow its speed. The waiting officers saw that it had as its passengers a man and woman.

Deputy Alcorn, who knew the outlaw, took a tight grip on his rifle.

"It's Barrow . . . that's the car!" he told his companions.

The auto moved closer . . .

The dark-eyed, black-haired young man at the wheel was talking to the girl at his side, remarking perhaps on the becoming red dress and hat she was wearing—something new that she had picked up only a few days before.

The young woman made some reply, as she put aside a half-eaten sandwich to open a package of cigarettes. But what was this—a man rising from the ditch at the side of the road?

Looked like Captain Frank Hamer, who used to live in Dallas when he was in the Rangers! Why, it was Captain Hamer, and he was shouting "Halt!" and pointing a rifle!

The dark-faced young man released the wheel, reached for the rifle between his knees; the young woman clutched the package of cigarettes a bit tighter, and gazed wide-eyed at the roadside. Other men were scrambling from the ditch.

And then something smashed into the windshield and side of the car, a violent swish of hail that came with a deafening roar. The road faded before the eyes of the young man and the girl. The world went suddenly black as the car swerved and hit the ditch.

Captain Hamer found Clyde Barrow resting against the door on the driver's side, the holes from fifty slugs through his body. One ear was shot away and his chest was terribly mangled.

Bonnie Parker, indescribably mutilated by the leaden volley from six rifles, was slumped forward in her place, still clutching the package of cigarettes in one hand, holding in the other the barrel of a shotgun. The red dress was redder now.

"As inured as I am to the slaughter of humans," said Hamer, later, "I was sickened by the sight of Bonnie's body nearly torn to pieces with bullets. Even though she was a killer, I felt a sinking at the pit of my stomach as I opened that car door and saw her."

But the captain says he remembered, as he sighted down his rifle at the approaching car, the scene on the Grapevine road . . . a woman standing over a fallen highway patrolman and pumping shots into his body.

"Anyhow," he added, "I hated to bust a cap on a woman."

A wrecker hauled the riddled car to Arcadia, the bodies within it, and Captain Hamer hurried to the telephone to make his report.

Chief Phares of the highway patrol sat at his desk

in Austin. The telephone bell tinkled and he picked up the receiver.

"Phares speaking," he said.

"This is Hamer, and I'm in Arcadia, Louisiana," came the voice at the other end of the wire. "We've done the job."

And that was all. The connection was broken. Hamer had hung up.

Chief Phares, who wanted details, had to put in a call to Louisiana and get the Arcadia operator to send down the street for the captain. Then he got the details —in characteristic Ranger fashion.

"There wasn't much to it . . . we set a trap . . . they ran into it and we sprung it . . . our rifle fire struck them in the heads at an angle . . . the car went into a ditch . . . neither of them said a word . . . they died with their mouths shut."

There wasn't much to it? Not much . . . except that a Ranger had met a gangster's challenge—and another chapter of service history written!

CHAPTER XXII

The Last Frontier

WE HAVE passed the last frontier. . . .

The Centaur of the Plains no longer rides the bloody trail, a noose of buckskin 'round his mustang's nose, a red-tipped lancehead flashing in the sun.

Those hostile tribesmen, the Comanche and the Kiowas, whose reign of fire and death and terror made necessary the organization of the first Frontier Battalion, were sent long years ago to live upon the reservation; but they remain, even to this day, under the watchful eyes of Uncle Sam's garrison at Fort Sill, Oklahoma.

Of the tribesmen, descendants of those warriors who met in the lodge of Sleeping Wolf to form the sinister confederacy of 1795, only a few are left—naught but the pitiable remnant of a once proud nation that dared defy encroachment of the white man on the happy hunting grounds.

Search the length and breadth of the Great Staked Plains, hunt the banks of the Pease, and explore the valleys of the Antelope Hills and you will never find in all that sea of grass and rolling prairie one Indian left upon the sites where once the tipis of his fathers stood. You might, if you are lucky, find a lance-head in a pile of rock, or an arrow mouldering in a mound of dust— small, grim reminders of a day when that wide land was called the devil's playground; tragic mementos of a race that fought . . . not wisely, but too well.

On these plains occurred the last sorrowful conflict between the forces of civilization and the hordes of savagery, with civilization triumphant in the end. None can deny that the fate of the red man was tragedy, and none can say whether the white man was justified in the course he took. The law of the Indian was one of the oldest—the law of survival for the fittest—and he put it into bitter execution when the white man began the slaughter of his buffalo. He faced annihilation and he fought back, using the only method of warfare that he knew, a method in which the tomahawk and scalping knife played leading rôles.

But if the Indians had a law the Texans didn't recognize it. They called it not a law, but a condition . . . a condition of savage atrocity, and to combat it the Rangers of the first six battalions went to the frontier to make laws and conditions of their own, carrying strapped about their waists in leather holsters the "six-chambered courts of authority" to punish without indictment and without trial.

These men were not from the riff-raff and the backwash of the more finished civilizations. They were hard, but they were gentlemen—seeking to mold from the raw material the finished product of a new country.

In the rout of the ponies and the subsequent defeat of Quanah in the battle of Palo Duro Canyon, General Ranald Slidwell Mackenzie and the regiment of cavalry he commanded at Fort Richardson in Jack County did much to mop up the last poor remnants of the Comanche nation and place the survivors on the reservation at

Fort Sill, but his was the clean-up job, the Texas Rangers
having laid the groundwork.

And the Indian hasn't forgotten. Only a few years
ago one of the last survivors among the captains who
fought across the hunting grounds, was walking through
the Mescalero reservation, and a companion noticed that
he glanced about as though looking for something. He
asked an explanation.

"Well," said the captain, "I'm sorta keeping an eye
out for Magoosh . . . the old chief knows who put him
here."

Today the broad stretch of country which lies
between the Pecos and Panhandle, and between Fort
Worth and the New Mexico line, is a land of fertile
fields and prosperous ranches, a great empire within
whose borders a civilized people may follow in safety
the pursuits of peace and happiness.

The Texas Rangers made it that way—captains courageous like Jack Hays, Coleman, Burleson, John Ford,
Sul Ross and Major Jones.

We have passed the last frontier—even along the hun-
dreds of Texas miles which dip into the Río Grande. No
longer do the big-spurred banditti ride across the border
to lift the Texas steers; no longer do harassed citizens
watch, helpless, as their herds diminish and then flee the
country to save their own lives.

The lesson that McNelly and Hughes and Frank Jones
taught on the river still holds good—that "one Ranger
is worth a hundred troops."

These were the two frontiers the Texas Ranger tamed,
the two frontiers which made him necessary. First the

Indians, then the banditti—though the proverbial Texas bad man, like John Wesley Hardin, did have his place in the picture. But even those two-gunned gentry knew the magic of the word "Ranger."

The notorious King Fisher, back in the '70s, laughed loud and long at local officials but when the Ranger, fondling the butt of a heavy revolver, tapped him on the shoulder in a Brownsville saloon, Mr. Fisher went along like any other black-fleeced lamb.

Sam Bass, from whatever place he occupies in the land of the hereafter, can testify to the accuracy of the Ranger's aim . . . likewise Seba Barnes.

—And the Rangers handled Wesley Hardin.

There is a tradition in the Rangers and they sensed it—Indian, Mexican and bad man all alike; and even in this day, when the law provides for only four field companies of fifteen men each, as compared with the old organizations which set out for the frontier with a muster roll of seventy-five or more, there still is magic in the word.

There is slight need today for many men, for Texas has become a decent place in which to live—her destiny having been carved out with powder, lead and the Bowie knife.

We have passed the last frontier, but at its borders stands a grim, gray figure, still on watch. A ghost from out the past, he wears upon his breast a shield, about his hips two heavy guns, upon his head—a big white hat.

INDEX